THROUGH A HEDGE BACKWARDS

A Memoir

Volume 1
Rats and Stats
Discovering Psychology in the Swinging Sixties

About this book
Enter the life of a 1960s psychology student.

"Rats and Stats" is based on a blog that has reached thousands of readers in many countries around the world and has been described by its readers as a *great read: interesting, entertaining, enjoyable and well written*.

This first volume of the "Through a hedge backwards" memoir series captures the life of a student of psychology at Queensland University in ultra-conservative Brisbane in the swinging sixties.

The author has an intimate knowledge of psychology in Australia and provides an insiders view of the development of the profession through its adolescent years. The book delivers a critical examination of the behind the scenes maneuverings to resolve the serious issues facing the profession, told against the backdrop of the social history of the times.

This critique of the history and politics of Australian psychology is leavened with controversial theories, anecdotes of student life, street marches, wild parties and the life of a singer songwriter. The author also introduces us to his sometimes-controversial teachers and his radical student friends.

But Ian has a secret problem. He is uncoordinated, half-blind, dyslexic and can't hold his drink. His struggle to overcome these hidden weaknesses is woven through his story with a light but thoughtful touch.

- Will Ian pass his exams and get a job or will he be arrested and beaten up in a protest march?
- Can Australian psychology escape the dominance of the medical profession and break away from the British Psychological Society?
- What is the complicated compromise governing the training of psychologists?
- Does Ian fulfill his dream to have his songs published on an album?
- Can he reconcile the scientific bent of the Psychology Department with his desire to be a practical, therapeutic psychologist?
- Can Ian survive on $10 a week and can he overcome his tendency to fall asleep when he drinks alcohol?

Read this memoir to find out.

'It draws the reader in.' – Frank McDonald

'I enjoyed the read and the laugh.' – George Tully

About the Author

Dr Ian Hills studied psychology in the sixties with MacElwain and his staff at Queensland University. For Ian the sixties was a formative time of change, fun and enlightenment. After graduating he practiced as an adventurous psychologist more or less continuously until his retirement.

Ian has taught and studied in universities in Australia, the UK and the USA, worked with remote Aboriginal groups, and been Director of Psychology in a major teaching hospital among many other roles. He has appeared as an expert witness at all levels of the Australian legal system and occasionally in the newspapers and on the radio.

His experience of psychology has ranged from the freewheeling sixties and seventies through the professionalisation of the eighties and nineties to the over-regulated noughties and teens.

He has a close involvement with the evolution of the field of psychology and is a participant in the events he describes. He took part in many of the decisions that shaped Australian psychology in the twentieth century and was a voice of dissention when Australian psychology took directions that he did not agree with. He resigned in protest from the Australian Psychological Society so many times that he was a non-member for nearly half of the 50 years of his professional life.

His protest activities were not confined to professional matters. He continues to be an active campaigner for the environment, peace and human rights.

Ian's activism is often reflected in the songs he writes and sings. As a friend once put it "Ian writes songs to scrape his shit off the walls and get it in a neat pile where he can deal with it".

Ian has been a family man and a divorcee. He has four children and numerous grandchildren who have enlivened his life and brought depth to his practice of psychology.

Ian is now retired and lives on a 25-acre bush property in a house he built himself. He spends his time writing, playing music and going on long exploratory drives through the Australian countryside.

He writes a popular blog "Through a hedge Backwards" at: http://psychologyinqueenslandmemoir.weebly.com/blog

Make contact

Email the author or receive notice of forthcoming books
http://psychologyinqueenslandmemoir.weebly.com/blog

THROUGH A HEDGE BACKWARDS

A MEMOIR

VOLUME 1
RATS AND STATS
DISCOVERING PSYCHOLOGY IN THE SWINGING SIXTIES

IAN HILLS

Published in Australia in 2016 by
Riverland Press
37 Scotneys Rd, Moolboolaman, Qld, 4671
http://psychologyinqueenslandmemoir.weebly.com/memoir.html

Ian Hills asserts the right to be identified as the author of this work
Copyright © Ian Hills 2016

All rights reserved. Apart from fair use no part of this publication may be reproduced, stored in a retrieval system, or transmitted in any form or by any means, electronic, mechanical, photocopying, recording, or otherwise, without the prior written permission of the copyright owner.

ISBN: 978-0-9953994-2-6

A CiP catalogue record for this book is available from the National Library of Australia

Cover photograph of the author by Frank McDonald
http://frankmcdonaldphoto.smugmug.com/
Cover photograph curtisia dentate hedge by Abu Shawka
https://commons.wikimedia.org/wiki/File: Curtisia_dentata_-_hedge_45.JPG
Cover icon by icons8 https://icons8.com/web-app/7403/psychology

For my family

I should not write so much about myself if there were anybody else whom I knew as well.

Henry Thoreau, Walden, 1854

Contents

Foreword by John Tomlinson 15
Preface 17
Acknowledgements 19
Introduction 21
Prologue 23

Chapter 1 **Background to the sixties and the foundations of   Australian psychology** 27
Chapter 2 **A place of light liberty and learning** 33
Chapter 3 **Trends shaping Australian psychology in the sixties** 35
Chapter 4 **Student life** 39
Chapter 5 **Psych on a bike** 43
Chapter 6 **The Suzuki and the gangster car** 47
Chapter 7 **Tensions shaping psychology in the sixties: psychology and medicine** 51
Chapter 8 **Finding my feet at university** 55
Chapter 9 **Learning to pass** 59
Chapter 10 **Generalising my exam passing method** 63
Chapter 11 **Learning my trade** 67
Chapter 12 **Dr Gordon Mangan** 73
Chapter 13 **Human beings and other animals** 79
Chapter 14 **Is there such a thing as human instinct?** 85
Chapter 15 **Culture and family** 91
Chapter 16 **Culture, civil rights and song writing** 95
Chapter 17 **John Tomlinson: radical student** 99
Chapter 18 **John Tomlinson: radical social worker** 105

Contents (*cont.*)

Chapter 19 **Ants and the death wish** 111
Chapter 20 **Getting hooked on science** 115
Chapter 21 **Laurie Enticknap and speed reading** 119
Chapter 22 **Statistical Encounters** 123
Chapter 23 **Professorial Influence** 129
Chapter 24 **More about Mac** 133
Chapter 25 **Measurement Theory** 137
Chapter 26 **Measurement and clinical practice** 141
Chapter 27 **The marvellous mind of John Keats** 145
Chapter 28 **Elsie Harwood and Clinical Psychology** 149
Chapter 29 **Test practice and mislaying a client at Goodna** 153
Chapter 30 **Elsie Harwood, clinical training and Operation Retirement** 157
Chapter 31 **Elsie Harwood and Psychological Testing** 161
Chapter 32 **Commem week pranks** 165
Chapter 33 **Further adventures in testing** 169
Chapter 34 **The Queensland Test and Cultural Fairness** 173
Chapter 35 **Critical decisions** 177
Chapter 36 **The autokinetic illusion and dreams** 181
Chapter 37 **My first teaching job and the legacy of Moorlands** 185
Chapter 38 **Teaching at Moorlands** 189
Chapter 39 **Graduation** 193
Epilogue 197
Note: **References, bibliographies, links and indexing** 199
Appendix: **Gordon Mangan's Bibliography** 201
Index 207

Foreword

Ian Hills' account of growing up in Brisbane, adjusting to life at university and coming to terms with the challenges of living in South East Queensland in the 1960s and seventies paints a picture which may be familiar to many of his readers yet which is haunting in its directness.

The book is written without pretence. Ian demonstrates a capacity for self-reflection without becoming self-absorbed. His training as a psychologist provides him with the tools to observe and describe what has been going on around him without becoming trapped by the minutiae.

He has had an interesting professional career as both an academic and practitioner and he does not shy away from the difficulties that seem to dog our paths as we struggle to live a meaningful life, whilst confronting obstacles which might tempt us to choose the low road.

Ian's account of the pressures he felt as a PhD student gives a good example of the difficulties faced by postgraduate students and the sacrifices which those around us make in order that the higher degree is obtained.

But he is more than a psychologist, he has written some beautiful songs, is an accomplished musician and singer and has attempted to enhance the cause of Aboriginal self-determination in many and varied ways.

His ability to sift through the detritus of life without getting lost amongst the zooplankton gives strength to his analysis. He can give shape to the important as a background to the mundane. I'm sure you'll enjoy the book.

Dr John Tomlinson PhD   Sydney, November 2016

Preface

I often wish that my parents had written a memoir. It was not the habit of that generation to discuss their lives and it was not the habit of mine to ask. But not knowing leaves gaps in ones sense of history and belonging that can be a constant itch.

I thought I could head off this intergenerational lack of knowledge by writing down my own personal history for my children and grandchildren. And so I started writing a memoir.

Later I needed a writing project to supply the necessary hours of professional development to maintain my registration as a psychologist. The memoir seemed an obvious choice since I had already started. I had found my voice and style and developed a productive writing habit. I refocussed my writing on my training and career as a psychologist so I could legitimately claim that it was psychological writing. And that's how my memoir became a personal history of psychology in the twentieth century.

I soon found that I was expressing opinions about events that I had participated in and which had influenced my future as a psychologist as well as telling stories about my life as a psychology student and describing my teachers and friends. The result was not exactly history, not exactly autobiography, not exactly critique but it has elements of all three, so I think it would probably qualify as memoir.

I found that others enjoying reading it as much as I enjoyed writing it. So I decided to publish the memoir as I went along to get broader and more regular feedback. That's how my memoir became a successful blog read by thousands in ten countries.

When I finally decided that I had written enough for a book and it was time to publish, I found I had enough material for two or possibly three books. I had only covered ten years of my life and I intend to continue writing about the other forty years of my career and the twenty or so years that fall on either side of it. And so the book has developed into a series. Thus my original intention of informing my descendants of my history has broadened to become a vehicle for informing my profession of an important era in the history of its development.

I haven't forgotten my original intention. The chapters describing the early years of my life are still in my computer waiting to be published as a prequel.

Ian Hills
Moolboolaman, November 2016

Acknowledgements

My thanks to the many friends, family and colleagues who have joined me on this journey - especially to those who have contributed comments and additional information to the story.

In particular my sincere thanks go to Frank Macdonald for his unflagging support of this project and his friendship over many years. Frank has also generously allowed me to use his photograph of me.

Thanks to those who have generously given me permission to write about them while placing no restriction on what I write.

John Tomlinson, along with his contributions, has continued a friendship of many years standing and reminded me of our days of song writing and radicalism in the sixties.

Mike Browning has spent many hours reading, analysing and discussing with me each chapter as it was written and George Tully has made many thoughtful observations. They have contributed greatly to clarifying and expanding my thoughts and by doing so constantly remind me of why I am making the effort to write.

My thanks also to John Ray who has carefully read each chapter and made useful comments and even linked and republished a couple of the chapters.

My long-suffering friends and family deserve a special mention for their willingness, without complaint, to discuss, read and reread sections of the manuscript. They have put up with my enthusiasm without appearing the least bit bored. They have spent their time and effort in proofing and improving my drafts. Thank you, your support has been crucial.

I am eternally grateful for the existence of the profession of psychology which has held my interest and nurtured me for more than 50 years and for the psychologists who preceded me on this journey which is far from over.

Introduction

Through a hedge backwards was the title of a long anticipated memoir that my mother sometimes threatened to write in the last years of her life.

She explained to me that one of her teachers at Reading University where she studied Education had often said to her *"Joyce, you look as though you have been through a hedge backwards"*. She loved the idea that it implied that she was strong willed and independent minded (which she was) and (metaphorically speaking) often could not be bothered with going through the gate that others used and instead would barge straight through the hedge, if necessary, against resistance, backwards. It's possible that her teacher meant only that she was untidy in appearance - a characteristic that I inherited. Unfortunately Mum never did get round to writing that memoir - a big pity, for she would certainly have imparted some important and unusual insights with good humour and biting wit.

I feel justified in appropriating her title for my own memoir because it is apt from both a personal and a professional perspective. My career has also been one of wilful independent mindedness with more that an untidy dash of *crash or crash through*. This characteristic has also been a strong undercurrent in the progress of Psychology as a profession in the latter half of the twentieth century.

Further justification for using this title, if one is needed, is found in a comment by one of my readers who wrote: *Couldn't think of a better title!! Perhaps it also aptly describes mankind's evolution or devolution through the ages! It calls for Leunig style cartoon I feel.*

In the early sixties, when psychology was focussed on defining itself as a scientific discipline, much of the course work centred on statistics and learning experiments with rats. Those of us who would rather have dealt more with people sometimes referred disparagingly to these courses as *rats and stats*. That phrase appealed to me as a good title for this first volume. It expresses one of the underlying tensions in the profession of psychology that originated around the time I am writing about and has continued ever since – the desire to be a strict scientific discipline versus the wish to be a practical therapeutic profession.

Of course not all of the courses were about animals and statistics and at Queensland University in particular there were some applied courses. Even so one gained a distinct impression that some of the other psychology departments, and some of my lecturers at Queensland University, tried hard make it all *rats and stats* against a tide of opinion to the contrary.

In this memoir series *Through a hedge backwards* I look back on the adventure that Psychology has been on in Australia (particularly Queensland) during the last fifty years, from the personal perspective of the part I played in it.

In this first volume *Rats and stats* I describe my life as a psychology student in the early sixties and examine the social setting and the tensions that have shaped the profession of psychology. On a personal level I write about my love life, my emerging career as a singer songwriter, wild parties, street marches and difficult decisions.

Prologue

At the beginning of 1962 I entered Queensland University with only vague ideas about my future and career. My tastes ran to music and literature, my mother's to psychology and social work. As usual, my mum was able to persuade me that she was right and I enrolled in a combined psychology/social work degree without much idea as to what lay ahead. That's how things were done in those days.

I had just come from a post-school working holiday on a pineapple farm near Montville, which was then a tiny village. I had spent many weeks of twelve-hour days on my hands and knees pulling crow's-foot grass by hand from between rough-leaved pineapples. It was backbreaking work and although I was glad of the money in my pocket I was more than ready to give up the farming life and move on to academia.

The contrast couldn't have been greater. I found the complexity of the St Lucia campus and the extent of my freedom dizzying. It took me some time wandering around the campus to find the refectory. It took even longer to find the classrooms I was supposed to turn up to once I had put my timetable together.

Within a few days I had found myself student digs and moved out of home.

I had scored myself a Commonwealth Scholarship (one of only 200 or so awarded), which paid for my tuition fees and books, but my parent's earnings were such that the scholarship did not allow for living expenses. My parents gave me an allowance of £5 a week (about $80 in today's money) and that, along with the money I had saved from my holiday jobs, got me through the academic year.

I was the only one of my siblings to attend university. My mother was university educated but my father was not. Academia was not much discussed in our house so I had very little idea of what to expect. I was all set to embark on a venture that I had no conception of. It was terrifying and exhilarating.

THROUGH A HEDGE BACKWARDS

A Memoir

Volume 1
Rats and stats

Discovering Psychology in the swinging sixties

Ian Hills

CHAPTER 1

Background to the sixties and the foundations of Australian psychology

For most of the sixties, Menzies led a conservative Government in Canberra, and Bjelkie Petersen led a conservative – and what was later found to be a corrupt - government in Queensland. There seemed to be no prospect of a liberal-leaning let alone a Labor-led government. People seemed content with that. The political and economic scene was stable, there was nearly full employment and even the poor were comparatively well off (unless they were Aboriginal). It was easy to find a job and it didn't seem possible that people could be unemployed if they didn't want to be. In my school and university holidays I worked at engineering shops, a butchers, a pineapple farm and sorting mail over Christmas. Employers were glad to take me on for a few weeks, gave me simple jobs and once they were sure I was coping left me to it. It didn't cross my mind that I wouldn't be able to turn my hand to such a variety of work, and apparently my employers also had few qualms about it. This buoyancy in the economic scene led to an entrepreneurial spirit in psychology that was fostered by my teachers and led to the somewhat adventurous approach of many psychologists of the seventies - including myself.

My teachers, the previous generation of Australian psychologists, had received their training and baptism of fire in the armed forces. According to Cooke (2000): *World War Two provided Australian psychologists with an unprecedented opportunity to demonstrate the value of their science.*

During WWII psychologists assisted in selection and placement of recruits and devised a visual landing system for aircraft. Perhaps their most lasting legacy of this time was the WOSB (War Office Selection Board) tests. These tests were designed to enable swift detection of officer material to replace the rapidly depleting upper class (who were of course automatically enrolled as officers)

Similar tests are still being used to this day but under a different acronym AOSB (Army Office Selection Board) and under a more egalitarian regime that now routinely selects officers on the basis of merit rather than class. The work of the new generation of scientific psychologists played no small part in bringing about this and other major shifts in social structure.

Prior to 1944 Australian psychologists wishing to affiliate with a professional body belonged to the Australian Association of Psychology and Philosophy. Psychology's accelerating move towards a more scientific approach meant that a split with philosophy was inevitable and since both groups felt that the Society was more philosophical than psychological it was psychology that moved out. Psychologists formed the Australian Branch of the British Psychological Society in October 1944, always with the intention of making it an Australian organisation as soon as possible. Some favoured joining with the Americans, since they were more established and more scientific, but in the end with America yet to enter the war the ties to Empire won out.

According to Cooke (2000) the association with the British society was an uneasy one from the start with the Australian Branch wanting to establish its own policy lines. For example, the Australian Branch wanted to have a University qualification as a prerequisite for membership and after a prolonged tussle the parent society finally relented and took the unlikely step of allowing one of its branches to set a higher entry level than their own. This was not the only difficulty between the two bodies, the tension being such that Cook (2000) describes the Australian Branch as *a wilful and unmanageable offspring* of the British Psychological Society.

Many of my psychology lecturers in the 1960s were ex-armed forces, part of the scientific movement in psychology and foundation members of the Australian Branch. They were the adventurers and entrepreneurs of a new discipline in a young country and it was their drive and integrity that established the foundations of psychology in Australia. Their values and approach had a profound influence on my development as a psychologist.

It's hard to describe, to those who did not experience it, what living in the sixties was really like. Even to those of us who were there it seems like another world. The popular adage: *if you can remember the sixties – you weren't really there* only begins to catch the flavour of the times.

At the beginning of the sixties the Establishment was securely in charge. By the end of the decade the challenge to old ways was firmly established. Everything was changing during those ten years. It was an exciting, dangerous, creative, frightening, wonderful decade to live in. At the time it felt like it would go on forever.

On the world stage Europe and the Pacific were just recovering from World War II. England had finally finished with rationing only a year or so before we migrated to Australia in 1959.

Menzies' attempt to have Communism outlawed by referendum had failed less than ten years before. When asked later in a retirement interview if he thought the referendum had been a political mistake, he replied, "the result was". Nevertheless the *reds under the beds* scare tactic continued to win elections for conservative politics for most of the sixties, and the tags *communist* and *fellow traveller* were used successfully to smear the reputations and damage the careers of left-leaning opponents of the status quo.

John Kennedy became president of the USA in 1960 and the civil rights movement received a boost from his courageous support. He was assassinated in 1963, and his brother Robert was killed in 1968, just after the civil rights activist Martin Luther King was also murdered. It seemed that the civil rights movement might flounder, but it continued to flourish in the USA and eventually in a muted way here in Queensland.

The world seemed constantly on the brink of annihilation through the deadly competition between the USA and the USSR to test and stockpile ever more dangerous atomic weapons. Later this race acquired the acronym MAD (Mutually Assured Destruction). We really did think the leaders of the world's biggest powers were at least on the verge of insanity. Some miracle held them back long enough to see sense. I never quite worked out what it was.

The Russians put the first man into space and the Americans put the first man on the moon and they narrowly avoided turning the space race into a space war.

The Beatles rose to meteoric stardom by introducing classical harmonies into popular music. It was a decade of singer-songwriters and I became one, writing love songs and protest songs which I sang at the very popular Tuesday lunchtime folk concert in the Social Sciences lecture theatre - the only space big enough to contain the huge crowds that attended week after week.

After a while this activity was accused of being a communist front and closed down. At our final lunchtime concert as a measure of protest we sang as many songs as we could containing the word "red". My contribution was "Red Sails in the Sunset".

Bibliography

Australian Psychological Society Archives, Historical note. (n.d.). Retrieved from http://gallery.its.unimelb.edu.au/imu/imu.php?request=multimedia&irn=4938

Australian Psychological Society Oral History Project. (1994). *History of Australian Science Newsletter,* 32. Retrieved from http://www.asap.unimelb.edu.au/hasn/no32/news32.htm

Boag, S. (2008). A Brief History Of Personality And Individual Differences Research In Australia. In: S. Boag (Ed.) *Personality Down Under: Perspectives from Australia.* Nova Science Publishers.

Cooke, S. (2000). *A meeting of Minds.* Brisbane: APS Ltd.

Coulter, A. (2010). A 50-year involvement in psychology. *Psych News,* March.

Day, R. (2013). *History of the Australasian Society for Experimental Psychology(ASEP), previously the Canberra Symposia in Perception.* Retrieved from http://www.asep.com.au/History%20of%20ASEP.htm

Leahey, T. H. (1994). *A history of modern psychology.* Englewood Cliffs, NJ: PrenticeHall.

Rubinstein, W. D. & Rubinstein, H. L. (1996). *Menders of the Mind - A History of The Royal Australian and New Zealand College of Psychiatrists, 1946–1996* [Google eBook]. Retrieved from http://books.google.com.au/books?id=NpB0EeJImAwC&source=gbs_navlinks_s

Links

Assassination of John Kennedy
http://en.wikipedia.org/wiki/Assassination_of_John_F._Kennedy

Assassination of Robert Kennedy
http://en.wikipedia.org/wiki/Assassination_of_Robert_F._Kennedy

Communism referendum,
1951http://en.wikipedia.org/wiki/Australian_referendum,_1951

The Beatleshttp://en.wikipedia.org/wiki/The_Beatles

Assassination of Martin Luther King Jr.
http://history1900s.about.com/cs/martinlutherking/a/mlkassass.htm

Joh Bjelke-Petersen
http://en.wikipedia.org/wiki/Joh_Bjelke-Petersen

Queensland Mental health Services - Historyhttp://www.health.qld.gov.au/mentalhealth/docs/qld-mh-history.pdf

CHAPTER 2

A place of light liberty and learning

Inscribed in the sandstone façade above the main entrance of the University of Queensland is the legend: *Place of light, liberty and learning.* The word on the campus in the sixties was: *the lighting is quite adequate.*

As for liberty? Nicklin was in power with the same right wing attitudes and values as the later better-known Bjelke-Petersen. It was Nicklin who managed to prolong the second Mt Isa Mines dispute in 1964 by using it as a reason to pass an unnecessarily harsh order in council extending police powers. This resulted in a breakdown of negotiations just as the union and the mine were reaching agreement and paved the way for even more repressive police power laws later in the decade.

And with regards to learning? Mr Pizzey had an interesting background for an education minister. His first education post was as a student teacher in a country school. In the early part of the 20th century, the student teachers were the backbone of the schooling system. Hand picked by their teachers from the brightest students they were assigned to teach under supervision without any formal teacher training and were subsequently examined and appointed as teachers. After a long stint as student teacher, Mr Pizzey eventually passed the exam and subsequently held two teaching posts over the following ten years. And then after a few years as an administrator in the Queensland board of Adult Education, he entered politics apparently with the aim of representing sugar cane farmers.

This was the man who was in charge of Education as I entered the hallowed front door of the University of Queensland to attend my first lecture on Social History. As one author writes: *With his educational background, Pizzey was appointed Minister for Education in Frank Nicklin's cabinet and retained this job for more than a decade. He was also deputy leader of the Country Party, but he took other concurrent roles also: he held the portfolios of migration (1960–68), Aboriginal and Islander affairs (1962–68) and police (1962–68). As education minister, Pizzey was praised for his focus on secondary schooling, although his sweeping intervention in education matters was considered to have led to Brisbane's first teachers' strike in 1968.* (Wikipedia)

I remember Mr Pizzey outlining, as the essence of Education policy, that within a few years he would be able to walk into any class room in Queensland and by knowing the time of day and what grade was being taught, he would know what the teacher would say next.

My mother – then principal of the Kindergarten Teacher's College and an educationalist of a high calibre – was of course appalled by this approach. She used to say that education philosophy ran in thirty-year cycles and Queensland was so far behind that it occasionally appeared to lead the world in educational thinking.

Mr Pizzey had oversight of University and all other education activities on Queensland including teacher training. In this role, he not only provoked Queensland's first teachers strike but also its first student teachers strike. I remember hearing the leader of the student-teacher's union denouncing Pizzey on the radio and appealing to lecturers to start treating student teachers as adults rather than children. He concluded with this unforgettable line: *This authoritarianism must be stamped out ruthlessly.*

What can I say? This was the educational climate in which I began my tertiary education. The lighting was adequate.

Links

Frank Nicklin

http://en.wikipedia.org/wiki/Frank_Nicklin

Jack Pizzey
http://en.wikipedia.org/wiki/Jack_Pizzey

Kindergarten Teachers College
https://www.qut.edu.au/about/our-university/history

CHAPTER 3

Trends shaping Australian psychology in the sixties

Unknown to me and most other first-year psychology students in 1962 the profession of psychology in Australia was facing a number of difficult challenges.

The professional body for Australian psychologists was still the British Psychological Society and the desire to break away and form an Australian Society was strong and had been stirring for some time. But resistance from more conservative members of the profession meant that it took considerable time to achieve. The formation of the Australian Psychological Society (APS) out of the Australian Branch of the British Psychological Society was a hot topic throughout my undergraduate years but the APS was not formed until 1966 – just in time for my graduation as a psychologist.

The second major challenge is still not completely resolved today. This was the rift between the *learned academic* psychologists who dominated the professional body and the *practical applied* psychologists who formed the bulk of the membership. Over the years this rift has expressed itself in the formation of a large number of breakaway groups that were established to represent the interests of the practicing psychologists. An attempt was made by the British Psychological Society to heal this rift by creating the Division of Clinical Psychology. The failure of this and similar moves over many years to bridge the gap between the academic and practical areas of the profession is attested to by the many hours of discussion and thousands of words written on the subject as well as the current existence of large breakaway groups such as the Federation of Private Practicing Psychologists of Australia and the Association of Private Practicing Psychologists of Queensland.

In the early sixties this rift was so profound that a senior Sydney academic sincerely advised me not to take up clinical psychology because it had no scientific basis and was, in fact, a fraud. I was shocked. But on reflection it did explain why at that time Sydney University had no applied programs and focused entirely on *rats and stats*. At Queensland University, by contrast, it was possible to take two full-year applied undergraduate courses – about the best you could do in Australia at the time. Psychology departments such as Queensland's, which offered applied courses, were looked down on as being unscientific and as a result had less influence within the Society.

It seems odd to contemplate that in those days it was not possible to take a higher degree in clinical psychology anywhere in Australia. Even today applied higher degrees in psychology are, falsely in my view, seen as of lower quality.

Of course, the accusation that applied psychology had a meagre evidence base had some foundation. But it turns out that this was mainly because the work was yet to be done – partly because applied research was seen as of lower quality and was therefore harder to fund and publish.

I am so glad that the proponents of Cognitive Behavior Therapy (CBT) broke that death spiral in the eighties and nineties and produced an avalanche of tediously meticulous evidence for CBT as a therapy. Inevitably other schools of therapy started to produce their own evidence of therapeutic effectiveness and clinical research was finally off and running. There are some things that I don't like about CBT but all is forgiven for that breakthrough in clinical research.

Even so the *learned academic* psychologists still contrive to look down on the *clinical and applied* psychologists and the rift continues, albeit with a slightly more level playing field.

Linked to this rift is the ongoing push by academic psychologists to increase standards - code for longer university training. Psychologists in the workplace argue that an increase in the qualifications required to practice psychology would inevitably lead to a sharp decrease in the number of psychologists graduating at a time when the demand for psychologists is rapidly increasing.

When I started my studies in psychology in 1962 a three-year degree was the entry standard for membership of the profession. My four-year degree was seen as slightly ahead of its time – the four-year degree requirement came in a little later. Obtaining a PhD was simply showing off and future-proofed my qualifications for the next 50 years.

The push for a postgraduate entry qualification now seems to have stalled and 50 years on most psychologists still enter the workplace with four-year degrees. There are several reasons for this. Higher degrees are expensive and the payback time in terms of extra wages earned seems to be much longer than any possible career trajectory. In addition, many four-year graduates do not qualify for entry into a higher degree course – their fourth-year marks are simply not good enough.

To encourage myself to continue with my PhD when my research had bogged down, I once calculated how much extra I would earn with my extra qualification over my lifetime. I worked out that the break-even point would come when I was 106 years old. After that it was all money for jam. I still continued with the PhD – I just stopped thinking about money.

Although the APS continues to push for higher entry standards this approach ignores the practicality that universities would be unable to supply the market demand for psychologists if the entry level was higher.

On the other hand, the Psychology Boards and the Australian Health Practitioner Registration Authority responsible for registering psychologists, have taken the view that most psychologists will continue to enter the workforce with four-year degrees. Their compromise position is that in the two years after graduation, whilst working, psychologists can be provisionally registered as long as they undertake a two-year program of study, of equivalent standard to a Masters level degree, supervised by an experienced psychologist. New registrants with a higher degree do not need this provisional period of extra study.

The result is an ungainly pull yourself up by your bootstraps procedure that satisfies no one, but nevertheless seems to work – and has for the last 20 years.

I'm not sure how this problem will eventually be resolved. Progress seems to have stalled. The Wikipedia entry for the Australian Psychological Society in 2013 contained a clear indication that this conflict is ongoing. Directly below the heading *Education and training* was an information box declaring:

The neutrality of this section is disputed. Please do not remove this message until the dispute is resolved. (May 2010)

The fact that the dispute remained unresolved for more than three years is an indication of how difficult the broader issues are to resolve and how problematic the solutions available.

At the time of writing in late 2016, the registration authorities continue to provisionally register psychologists with a four-year degree and fully register them after two years under supervision. The Australian Psychological Society, continues to grant associate membership to psychologists with a four-year degree plus two years practice under supervision, and full membership only to those with a Masters or Doctorate degree.

The friction between these two bodies over qualifications and other issues continues and is described in the 2016 Wikipedia entry for the Australian Psychological Society:

As of 2010 the Psychology Board of Australia became the sole agency responsible for the registration of psychologists across Australia. The transition to this new body has caused significant friction within the profession as it is overseen by a government controlled executive who have made decisions at odds with previous professional practice.

One solution is for a massive injection of funds into postgraduate psychology training – unlikely in the current economic climate. Another possibility is to install another level – assistant psychologists - to provide the numbers needed. This has been proposed and rejected before. Of course it is always possible (shock, horror!) to lower the entry standard. That is unlikely to be seriously proposed. Alternately employers might decide that the two-year investment in training does not give a sufficient return and stop employing entry-level psychologists.

I await developments.

Bibliography

McNamara, J. R. (1981). Some unresolved challenges facing psychology's entrance into the health care field. *Professional Psychology*, 12(3), 391-399.

Link

Australian Psychological Society. Retrieved from http://en.wikipedia.org/wiki/Australian_Psychological_Society

CHAPTER 4

Student life

My first year at University was a formative time when I learned the basics of academic life that formed the foundation for the next 50 years of my career, and considerably broadened my life experience

I lived in a share house in West End for a while and learned about the bohemian lifestyle that many students affected at the time.

From there I could ride my pushbike up Highgate Hill past the only high-rise in Brisbane and coast down to the river to catch the St Lucia Ferry. I became very good at timing my arrival to the departure times of the ferry, often arriving just in time to be the last person aboard. This was helped by the fact that I had a clear view of the river from the top of the hill and I could see the progress of the ferry across the river and time the speed of my descent accordingly. As my timing became finer my speed increased day by day until it became obvious that I would need new brake blocks in order to avoid running at full speed into the side of the ferry at the bottom of the hill.

And so it was that one morning, running exceptionally late but confident of my new brake blocks, I was speeding down the hill at a very fast rate when a car backed unexpectedly from an obscure driveway into my path. I had no time to swerve so relying fully on my newly acquired ability to stop I applied front and back brakes as hard as I could. Imagine my surprise to hear a ping from behind me quickly followed by another ping from in front as the brake blocks flew out of their housing and disappeared. My bicycle crashed into the side of the car but I managed an acrobatic leap over the top and continued careering down the road as fast as I could run. When I could stop running I returned to the car where the apologetic driver offered me a cup of tea and a new bike. I regretfully explained that the bike was a wreck anyway and a replacement could probably be found at any garbage dump, but I would be grateful if she could arrange for disposal of the mangled pieces of bike. I was just glad that she took full responsibility and I didn't have to pay for repairs to the car. I was late for the early lecture that day.

That night we held the most extraordinary party during which one of my housemates descended the quick way out of the lounge room window down a long way onto a pile of rocks.

The day before the party his girlfriend dumped him and he arrived home early and sat in the lounge room steadily drinking his way through several bottles of OP rum. We prepared for the party around him and he was a silent malevolent presence at the centre of the house as the guests started to arrive. Several unsuccessful attempts were made to get him to go to bed but he was having none of it. He was sure that his recently ex-girlfriend would attend the party and he was determined to stay awake and have it out with her. We began to hope that she would see sense and not turn up, or if she did he would have drunk himself to sleep first. We began to plan for eventualities.

Several hours later I noticed that the chair he had occupied in the middle of the lounge room was vacant. Hoping he had finally succumbed to sleep I checked his room. Then I started asking people if they had seen him in the last few minutes. I was informed that he was last seen sitting precariously on the window ledge and had refused to budge. I looked out the window to see his form spreadeagled face down on the only pile of rocks in the garden below. It was a long way down. I raised the alarm and then tried to work out how to get to him.

The house was typical cheap student accommodation – a very old Queenslander in a low market area perched precariously on the steep banks of the Brisbane River. The only way into the garden was via a precarious staircase at the outside of the back of the house, which no one had ventured to use in living memory. It was probably installed as a fire escape at some stage in the distant past and was dangerously rickety.

The alternative that suggested itself to me was to climb down the cliff on which the house was perched and that is what I did – at some risk to myself. I had no idea how I was going to retrieve him when I reached him, but I felt that some attention from my sketchy first aid skills would be better than nothing.

When I arrived at the base of the cliff I was alarmed and then mystified to find that the body had disappeared. I searched around the base of the house and eventually noticed my housemate half way up the rickety staircase. He was preceded and enticed upward by his ex-girlfriend who gave him encouragement (unwisely I thought) by blowing kisses. The remaining guests were crowded onto the veranda, shouting encouragement.

I watched with my heart in my mouth as they slowly ascended expecting at any moment that the stairs would collapse or at the very least the rail would give way as he lurched drunkenly against it, or that the whole structure would collapse sending the veranda, guests and all down on top of me.

They eventually arrived safely at the top to cheers and congratulations leaving me below in the garden wondering whether it would be more dangerous to climb the cliff or the stairs. I can't remember which I decided to do, or whether the hapless couple reunited after their adventure, but I can remember that my flatmate did not seek medical attention and seemed none the worse for wear in the morning. Not even a hangover! There is an old wives tale about drunks and babies and their immunity from injury. It could be true.

After that adventure I decided that the bohemian lifestyle was not for me and I found myself a quieter flat in South Brisbane, which I shared with a number of mostly uneventful flatmates. The exceptions were a young man with epilepsy who caused a moderate amount of excitement during his stay; a sociopath who left with two months unpaid rent, three of my new shirts and my guitar; and a bible college student who I tried to discourage from trying out his weekly evangelism assignments at the breakfast table. He was later posted to New Guinea where he devoted his life to translating the bible and bringing the dubious benefits of civilisation to an endlessly forgiving mountain tribe.

There was a lot of growing up to do between lectures, pracs, assignments and exams and living on $10 a week was far from easy, but all things considered it was a good life with few responsibilities and considerable personal freedom.

CHAPTER 5

Psych on a bike

After my pushbike accident at Highgate hill (see Chapter 4 *Student life*) I used public transport for quite a while and like most other Brisbane commuters found it very frustrating.

Most of the public transport services in Brisbane and many other cities are planned radially. That is to say the routes run from the centre of the city to the outskirts. This means that if you want to travel round the circumference of the city a journey of a few kilometres can take hours by public transport because you can only go to the centre of the city on one service and out to your destination on another.

I was very keen to own my own transport but I had to wait until the end of the year when I could get a holiday job and make some money. That year I worked two jobs simultaneously during the vacation – at an engineering shop during the day and in the mail exchange sorting mail at night – in order to make enough money to buy a motor bike. By the end of the vacation I was exhausted but had amassed enough money to buy a decent bike with some money left over for the year's expenses.

The bike I bought was a little beauty: a very old Ariel with a sidecar. It was powered by an engine with one huge 500cc cylinder that ran so slowly and powerfully that you could almost count the firing cycles. The sidecar was a big advantage: it was much more stable than bikes normally are (although it cornered strangely) and my girlfriend could ride in comfort in the sidecar more or less out of the wind and wet.

The salesman told me that it was an ex-police bike and was known for its power and speed. It certainly looked the part – shiny black and chrome with ornate gold speed-stripes - but I found it hard to imagine the cop in the sidecar being able to maintain his professional aplomb. Its top speed was well below the speed limit.

Nonetheless, there is a police archive photograph showing bikes with sidecars that look very much like the one I owned in the sixties, on display at the first police garage in Brisbane in 1936 at:

http://mypolice.qld.gov.au/museum/2013/10/08/from-the-vault-a-history-of-police-motorcycles/

I must say that the policemen in the sidecars in this picture seem to be struggling to maintain their gravitas. Apparently these bikes were used to convey forensic scene of crime experts to crime scenes. This was considered a major innovation that saved a lot of time. Previously forensic teams had used public transport to get to crime scenes.

A unique innovation on the Ariel police bike that I have not seen on any other vehicle was an advance-retard lever on the handlebars that could be used to change the engine timing as it ran. I could retard the firing to give the bike more power uphill and advance it to give it more speed on the flat. I used it to good advantage on the Bald Hills flats on the way home.

The Bald Hills stretch was a nightmare for motorcyclists on a cold winters' night when the temperature was hovering around freezing point and the wind-chill factor was excruciating. After a few weeks of nightly suffering I started to get arthritis in my knees. I counteracted this by stuffing the front of my trousers with the day's newspaper. This rendered the newspaper almost unreadable, but left my knees as warm as toast. It was effective enough for me to extend the technique to my upper body by stuffing the front of my jumper with newspaper too. It was years before I saw motorcycle leathers and realised that they were designed for just this problem. By that time it was too late – I already had a car.

The police bike gave me freedom I had not experienced before. I found it much easier to get from lectures in George St in the city to the St Lucia campus, and made the trip in record time – much like forensic scene of crime teams. At the weekends I travelled far and wide around Brisbane, even going to Stradbroke Island over a long weekend.

The trip to Stradbroke nearly did for the police bike and got me into trouble with my girlfriend's parents. I thought it would be a good idea to follow the four-wheel-drives down on to the surf beach and go for a drive along the sand. This worked well and we had a great time zooming along the coast at low tide, stopping for a picnic and returning in good time to catch the barge back to the mainland.

We would have been in good time if it were not for the soft sand on the climb up from the beach to the headland. The police bike stalled in the soft sand and then bogged. Not being as heavy as a car we were able to push the bike and sidecar up the loose sand dune riding the clutch to help us along. By the time we got to the top we were exhausted and the clutch was emitting clouds of acrid smoke.

With still a couple of hours to go before the last barge left I thought we had plenty of time to allow the clutch to cool before setting off across the island. However, when we mounted up, the engine roared, the clutch smoked, but the bike did not move.

We missed the barge and had to wait a day for new clutch plates to be delivered from the mainland. I soon replaced the plates and we set off, a day late, for home.

The early sixties were a strait-laced time and my future parents-in-law were not impressed that I had spent the night unsupervised with their daughter. They would have been even more displeased if they had realised that we spent the night sleeping rough on the beach.

The police bike went well for some time but eventually started to show its age. I replaced small bits successfully but when the wiring started to deteriorate I was out of my depth. I jerry wired the headlight and the horn but as the insulation around the wires began to fall off in small chunks I realised that I would have to replace the entire wiring harness.

I purchased a wiring diagram and took the petrol tank and some panels off the bike to expose the wiring harness. One look was enough. On the wiring diagram the wires were all nicely spaced so that it was easy to see what connected to what. Under the tank was a lizard like bunch of some 50 wires tightly bound together, with smaller clusters of wires entering and leaving, apparently at random, to unknowable destinations.

I reluctantly decided that it was time to trade in the police bike and move on to a newer model.

Link

Police bikes with sidecars
http://mypolice.qld.gov.au/museum/2013/10/08/from-the-vault-a-history-of-police-motorcycles/

CHAPTER 6

The Suzuki and the gangster car

After the demise of the police bike my next bike a Suzuki 80k was a completely different beast: much lighter and with a tiny engine it was manoeuvrable and reliable. I rode it everywhere and it lasted until I had my first and only accident.

The Suzuki's main disadvantage was that its narrow wheels were a perfect fit for the tramlines that ran along many of Brisbane's major roads. It was a significant hazard. I learnt how to negotiate tramlines by taking care to cross them at as steep an angle as possible. Running along parallel to the lines could mean that the wheels would catch in the track. Then any attempt to change direction would result in a dangerous wobble at least, and at worst a tumble.

One day as I was negotiating the long steep hill on the Newmarket road it began to rain. Rain is the worst weather for motorcycling and usually I would stop and put on my raingear. This day I was running late and it was only a light drizzle and I had just got to the sweet spot in my run up to the hill. Stopping would mean starting on the hill and a long slow ride to the top. I decided to keep going.

Halfway up the hill I encountered two trucks, overloaded and moving at a snails pace. I would either have to slow down to walking pace or overtake the trucks. The road was four lanes wide and there was plenty of room, so I took a quick decision to overtake both trucks.

I did a smooth lean to the right and started my run around the first truck. Unfortunately I had misjudged the distance to the top of the hill and the relative speed of the trucks so after overtaking the first truck I realised that I would have to pull in between the two trucks for the trip down the far side of the hill or risk overtaking the second truck at the top of a blind crest. I really did not like that idea but I was stuck with it.

As I started to pull in between the trucks disaster struck. I did a sharp lean to the left and my front wheel caught in the tram track. The bike fell flat and I tumbled off.

When I regained consciousness a few seconds later I opened my eyes to see the wheels of the truck swishing past a few inches from my head, one after the other. Swish, Swish, Swish, Swish... For a few nightmare seconds I lay there, not sure if I was under the truck or beside it. I was too frightened to move in case I moved under the wheels of the truck.

And then it was over. I had a very narrow escape.

I picked up the bike and walked it shaking to the side of the road. I could not bring myself to ride the bike again. As I stood there wondering what to do I noticed a second hand car dealer's yard at the bottom of the hill and without giving it much thought I walked the bike down to the yard and sold it for whatever they would give me.

Apart from a very short test run many years later I have never ridden a motorbike again.

Fortunately for me I was able to acquire a car shortly afterwards. It was a very old car rather like the ones you see in American gangster movies of the thirties. It had large wheel arches over the front wheels and a running board each side. It looked very like the picture of a 1936 Plymouth on this site:

http://www.autotrader.com.au/cars-for-sale/1936-PLYMOUTH-P2-SEDAN-JCW3879130/

For the first time petrol became a noticeable item in my budget for this car was a ferocious gas-guzzler.

That gangster car seemed to attract attention of the worst sort. Soon after I acquired it one of my radical friends suggested that it was the ideal car for a getaway after blowing up the new guardhouse at the entrance to the University.

The University authorities had recently decided that the solution to the campus parking problem was to prevent students from parking near the buildings. To achieve this they had built a barrier and a guardhouse at the entrance to the University. My friend proposed blowing up the guardhouse as a measure of protest. Needless to say I refused to be any part of this dangerous and harebrained plan and in any case I'm not sure he was serious in suggesting it. On the other hand it's nice to fantasise that I may have averted University of Queensland's first terrorist plot.

The car continued to serve me for some years but concluded its association with me as it had begun - with the worst sort of attention. The gangster car was stolen and taken for a joyride and later was found wrecked. The last service I performed for it was to remove it from the roadside and tow it to a wrecking yard.

Link

The gangster car
http://www.autotrader.com.au/cars-for-sale/1936-PLYMOUTH-P2-SEDAN-JCW3879130/

CHAPTER 7

Tensions shaping psychology in the sixties: psychology and medicine

A major challenge faced by psychologists in the early sixties was a heavily disguised but nonetheless ferocious turf war with the medical profession. In the sixties the medical profession by and large rated professions such as psychology, social work, physiotherapy and podiatry as only slightly less dangerous and offensive than chiropractic, homeopathy and naturopathy. All were lumped into the same discredited category as *alternative* - code for *fake* or *snake oil*.

The public argument between medicine and other health disciplines in the early sixties often centered on evidence for effectiveness. However, once the proponents of clinical psychology began to do their homework it became apparent that the average psychologist knows a great deal about evidence base, having spent at least four years studying the scientific method. In public forums psychologists were able to point out that many medical practices also had no scientific evidence base.

By the eighties the grounds of the argument began to shift as medicine began to loose ground. Concurrently there was a change in terminology from *alternative* to *complementary*. It sounded like a compliment but nobody was quite sure what it was code for.

It turns out that the stoush was not really about evidence at all. It was really about power. This became clear when the argument about evidence-base tailed off and the issue was worked out on the basis of industrial muscle. McNamara explains it like this in his 1981 paper:

...total medical authority over all health-related professions is sought. This medical dominance is inimical to the emergence of psychology as an independent health-related discipline. These differences are further magnified at a professional level, as psychology expands the scope of its practice and threatens the economic and organizational control that medicine exerts over health care.

The conflict between psychology and medicine can be traced back to at least the early 1900s. Simpson (2001) points out that a 1914 paper by Binet and Simon is a thinly veiled attack on the authority of medical profession.

Currently shadowing this unfinished discussion is the awful recent history of neglect and irresponsibility of some psychiatrists in charge of mental health facilities. The Ward 10B scandal in Townsville in the eighties, where a commission of enquiry found that the care and treatment of patients was *negligent, unsafe, unethical and unlawful* is a case in point.

At the Chelmsford Hospital in Sydney during the sixties and seventies, twenty-six patients died while undergoing deep sleep therapy with ECT. Exacerbating the dismay of this revelation was the news that the psychiatrists carrying out this treatment had been informed that there was no evidence for its effectiveness, but they continued to use it.

And lurking in the background is the worldwide ban on prefrontal lobotomies imposed in the seventies after it was discovered (why was this a surprise?) that it resulted in severe and irreversible brain damage.

The struggle is not over, but definite inroads have been made. It is now almost possible for a profession other than medicine to have overall responsibility for patient care in a mental health setting. On the other hand each time this occurs is a separate battle. There is no across the board or policy agreement on this.

Attitudes of the medical profession have mellowed considerably in the last 50 years. The era of the God-doctor ended some time ago and medicine as a profession has agreed to acknowledge some benchmarks set by others. It is now much more common to find medical practitioners interested in and valuing the practices of other health professions. These days medicine is more likely to function as part of a health team. But medical practitioners still like to be in charge of the team.

Psychology as a profession has made some concessions to enable its members to work in a medical setting. It allows members of the medical profession to have the final say in the treatment of its patients in hospital settings. It has adopted a curious double vision with regard to diagnosis so that the categorical diagnosis system of the medically based Diagnostic and Statistical Manual sits uncomfortably alongside the psychological perspective that each psychological attribute is a continuum that ranges through normal to abnormal at both extremes.

During the last 100 years rivalry has moderated into a working alliance. One can only hope that things continue to improve.

While I was a first year student these tensions within psychology were bubbling away in the background but were rarely noticed by the students. Occasionally disagreement occurred between staff members of opposing factions, but generally psychological professionals behaved professionally and kept their arguments to themselves.

These professional tensions - academic-practical, medical-psychological and improving standards – have been a constant background to my 50 year career in psychology and seem likely to be the backdrop to the development of psychology over the next 50 years.

Bibliography

Anderson, I. (1991). Nightmare on Chelmsford, Sydney. *New Scientist magazine,* 1750.

Binet, A. & Simon, T. (1914). *Mentally defective children* (W.B. Drummond, Trans.). London: Edward Arnold.

McNamara, J. R. (1981). Some unresolved challenges facing psychology's entrance into the health care field. *Professional Psychology*, 12(3), 391-399.

Simpson, M, K. (2001). Medicine vs. Psychology: The Emergence of a Professional Conflict in Development Disability. *Journal on Developmental Disabilities*, 8(2), 45–59. Retrieved from http://www.oadd.org/publications/journal/issues/vol8no2/v8n2download/vol8no2.pdf

Wilson, E. (2003). Psychiatric abuse at Chelmsford Private Hospital, New South Wales, 1960-1980s. In C. Coleborne and D. MacKinnon (Eds.), *Madness in Australia: histories, heritage and the asylum (pp. 121-134)*. Brisbane: University of Queensland Press.

Links

Australian Psychological Society. (n.d.). Retrieved from http://en.wikipedia.org/wiki/Australian_Psychological_Society

CHAPTER 8

Finding my feet at university

The Queensland University lecturing staff was generally of high calibre and made valiant attempts to sidestep any restrictions on liberty and learning and keep the academic, political and personal differences concealed. Although many did not hold PhDs they were mostly dedicated to teaching their subjects well and most, at least nominally, were enrolled in higher degrees.

For my first lecture in the main building – having passed under the yoke of *light, liberty and learning* – I joined other fledgling students to be instructed in Social History. The lecturer was a junior (though not young) staff member who struggled to present his material in a politically acceptable manner. He also struggled to be heard at times.

Not that the students were rowdy – far from it. We wouldn't have dared. The noise problem emanated from a blind student who contrived to take notes on what sounded like a homemade braille machine. Every minute or so the lecturer was interrupted by a series of ear-splitting clacks indicating that braille was being produced by hammering a spike through cardboard onto a metal plate. It is a mark of the politeness of the times that this was never complained about or even commented on.

At the end of the year the Social History lecturer concluded his lecture series with two apologies. First that he had been unable to fire us with revolutionary outrage at the social injustices that had occurred during the agrarian and industrial revolutions. Second that he was not allowed to present any Australian History, which he thought would have been of far more use and relevance to us.

Politically his remarks reflected the quietly emerging resistance to social restriction that permeated the university in the early sixties and would later break out in street marches and political demonstrations.

On the other hand he was well ahead of his time with regard to the teaching of history in Australia. It would be many years before the Rum Rebellion and the Eureka Stockade would be considered as proper history and some time before the concept of *oral history* was sufficiently accepted to allow Aboriginal history to enter the main stream.

In retrospect it seems amazing that I could have received instruction in history in Australia, first at school and then at university, and not been taught any Australian history. Even more amazing when you consider that having migrated to Australia only a few years before, my family set out to learn as much as possible about our adopted country. We immersed ourselves in Australiana. We sang Aussie folk songs, read Nino Culotta's *They're a Weird Mob* and learned how to cook sausages over an open fire. But when it came to Australian history we were so vague that we weren't sure if Ned Kelly was a real man or a composite myth like Robin Hood.

What I now know of Australian history comes from my own reading and most of this information was acquired much later in my life.

Most of my first year subjects were taught in the main building – perhaps because it had the largest lecture rooms. There I also attended lectures in Psychology, French, Philosophy and Preparatory German. So in all I started out with five subjects. A first year subject load was only supposed to be four but I was interested in so many things that I found it hard to cut it down to four. I decided that the best plan was to enrol in five and drop out of the one I enjoyed least. As it turned out I dropped out of two and had to catch up a subject in the following year.

These subjects left very little impression on my memory. I can remember some of the experiments in the first year Psychology course – plotting the areas of colour vision on the retina, and two-point sensitivity of the skin for example – but little of the lectures except that there was an awful lot of mathematics – a subject which, fortunately, I rather enjoyed.

I often wonder if the enduring emphasis on statistics in first year psychology represents an attempt to frighten off the wrong sort of student early in the course. If that happened psychology would then be left with the more scientific minded students, while the more "touchy-feely" students would be channeled into Social Work. Deliberate or not, that seemed to be the effect on my first year class and by second year we were already being molded into the fussy, obsessive scientists we were to become.

I recall that the professor of French had a cleft palate, which I came to regard as the best example of overcompensation that I was ever likely to come across when I learned about that concept from my psychology lectures. I also recall that I came close to failing a French assignment when I translated one of Montaigne's essays as though it had been written by a modern journalist for the front page of the Courier Mail. I thought I had made a humorous attempt to enliven a rather pedestrian piece of translation. The marker's comments indicated that what I had achieved was close to sacrilege.

Just a few months before I had qualified to take French at University level by passing the Senior (matriculation) exam in French at high school. The written test went well, but the dictation test was read by a young lady not long arrived in Australia from the depths of Scotland. Her accent was so thick that I had difficulty understanding her instructions in English, let alone her dictation in French. I have no idea how I, or any of my classmates, merited a pass for that dictation. We could only decipher a few random words. Perhaps this explains my rather cavalier approach to French translation. I found it hard to take French seriously after hearing it spoken with an unintelligibly broad scots accent.

Years later a colleague commiserated with me about the mangling of the French language by recalling that he had learned French in the United States with a fellow student from Texas who thought it was a great joke to say "Je parl Fransay avec un accent Texern mantenow." I guess you had to be there.

Philosophy started with a whole term, or was it a whole year, of logic. Perhaps that was also an intentional ploy to frighten away unsuitable students. I was an unsuitable student and dropped out after only a few weeks. I omitted to cancel my enrolment – I'm not sure that I even knew that I could – and so my academic record indicates that I am a failed philosopher.

I found that Preparatory German did not suit my needs for two reasons. Firstly I discovered that six months spent as a child in Swabia in southern Germany had prepared me for speaking and writing German about as well as six months spent in Wales would prepare a German child for speaking and writing Standard English. Swabian and Hoch Deutsch (proper German for *proper German*) turn out to be almost mutually unintelligible.

Secondly the lecturer reminded me far too much of the sadistic Swabian schoolmaster who conducted at least one savage beating a week in the class of the village school that I attended in the 1950s. I decided that Preparatory German was not the easy ride that it had promised to be either intellectually or emotionally and I dropped out with few regrets.

My first year was not the waste of time that the preceding description seems to imply, far from it. I passed three subjects and decided to devote my life to psychology (or perhaps social work) at some point during that year.

During that year I also learned a lot. I learned how to live on $10 a week (equivalent of about $80 in today's money), how to smoke cigarettes (a lot cheaper in those days) and that I really didn't enjoy alcohol much. Somewhere there probably still exists a photo captioned *Ian attempting to rise to the level of a coffee cup*. The problem (or perhaps benefit) still exists for me today – alcohol puts me almost immediately to sleep. Not the best position from which to enjoy a party. So although I became almost immediately addicted to nicotine the demon drink has never been a problem.

The downside of my predicament with alcohol was the way it restricted my social life. There was really no point in accepting an invitation to the Regatta if it meant falling asleep in the middle of a deep intellectual discussion in the early afternoon. The upside is that my liver is still more or less intact.

In my first year at university I learned to live independently – if being supported by your parents and a scholarship can be counted as being independent. I also passed enough subjects to be allowed to enrol in second year.

Bibliography

O'Grady, J. writing as Nino Culotta. (1957). *They're a Weird Mob* (republished). Australia: Penguin Books.

CHAPTER 9

Learning to pass

During my first year at university I learned to extend my idiosyncratic way of passing exams to the university level and to work out a way of not failing written assignments.

At school I had developed a way of overcoming my poor visual memory and very poor coordination in order to pass essay style exams. That particular combination of disability meant that at the best of times my handwriting was untidy and my spelling somewhat arbitrary. Under exam conditions what I wrote was more or less unintelligible.

A succession of teachers had tried without success to improve my handwriting with methods ranging from wrist loosening exercises (which had no effect at all) to rewriting essays neatly – which in fact made matters worse as boredom and fatigue set in. One by one they retired frustrated leaving me to my own devices. No one seemed to notice or care that I could not spell until it came time for matriculation. For the matriculation exam my headmaster advised me to break my arm and let him arrange to have someone write for me.

I devised what I thought would be a more permanent solution – after all I couldn't go breaking my arm every year at the same time indefinitely. I was quite accident prone but that would be stretching credibility.

It is a reflection of the changing times that in those days a broken arm was a respectable disability that called for assistance at exam time whereas poor coordination and a spelling disability was not. These days it is possible to get help for children with specific learning disabilities and in my role as a psychologist I have organised it on a number of occasions. In those days I was lucky that my mother was an expert in the education of children and recognised the wide streak of specific learning disability that runs in our otherwise high-functioning family.

By the time I became aware of such things my mother had apparently given up on improving my father's writing - he was in any case thriving quite nicely as a design draftsman without the use of written English. When called on he could print quite neatly. He even printed his signature.

My mother turned her attention and considerable skill to ensuring that her children were equipped with basic written survival skills. In my case it meant that I arrived at university with my self-esteem intact and a conviction that it was up to me to make sure that I was understood regardless of the illogicality of English spelling and the inaccuracy of my coordination.

In later years my mother ran a privately operated school for learning disabled children. Proudly displayed in the waiting room was a framed letter from me that I had written to her from Germany when I was nine. It was captioned: *Mothers take heart. The writer of this letter has just been awarded a PhD.* The letter was completely unintelligible – even to me.

In the sixties examinations were entirely of the essay type and required legible handwriting and accurate spelling regardless of the level of knowledge otherwise displayed. If the examiner couldn't understand what was written the examiner couldn't mark it – end of debate.

The currently used multiple guess exam style would have been a much better for me because it tests recall rather than expression and requires only a circle around the appropriate answer rather than a series of written sentences. Even though I deplore the current educational fashion for multiple-choice exams because they seem to have dumbed down critical thinking and erudite expression even among university graduates, I sometimes wish it had come into vogue some 20 years sooner. My early life would have been a lot easier if yearly exam essays had not been the only benchmark of ability.

My solution to poor handwriting and spelling involved a fairly simple idea: if my illegible answers were preceded by a neatly printed properly spelled dot point summary, examiners could get a fair idea of the quality of my knowledge and reasoning without having to struggle with my illegible handwriting. Since more or less readable printing was possible for me only if I was laborious and slow, I allocated half the time for each exam question to printing the summary and the other half to writing the essay as fast as I could. The essay was unintelligible but would have been anyway so nothing was lost there. The summary was easy to read so gave me the advantage of presenting something that was understandable.

I started developing this system when I was 16. Later at university I added some refinements. By then the neat summaries were based on my study of the textbooks and previous exam papers and I committed them to memory by using verbal mnemonics. For example, my summary for this blog so far might be:

Problems with writing and spelling
Coordination
Visual memory
Failing exams
Solved by
Neat summary
Based on study

The mnemonic would be based on the initial letters of each dot point: *P C V F S N B* and might be a nonsense sentence using words starting with these letters, for example: "*P*ercy *C*an *V*alue *F*at *S*ally's *N*ifty *B*ag". I would memorise the nonsense sentence by repeating it out loud – thus relying on my verbal skills rather than my less acute visual skills. I would practice setting myself exam questions and then writing out the letters of my mnemonic and expanding it into my neat summary thus making my practice a replica of the exam situation.

For each exam I developed a series of summaries to suit the questions I predicted would be asked – that is the questions I would have asked if I were an examiner. For most exams I memorised ten to fifteen answers for the six or so questions on the paper and I rarely had to make up a summary on the spot.

Having spent as much time as needed to write the clear summary of my answer, I then wrote as fast as I could for the remaining time allocated for that question and then printed neatly *out of time* before turning a page and starting on the next question. A bit cheeky – but it worked. In that way my answers would consist of a neat and concise summary followed by several pages of almost unintelligible scrawl expanding the summary. I'm almost certain that no examiner ever tried to decipher much beyond the summaries.

CHAPTER 10

Generalising my exam passing method

My method of passing exams seemed to work at school – at least sufficiently well to obtain a Commonwealth Scholarship to university. At university it became easier because I was in weekly contact with the examiners and it was easier to predict what they considered the most important areas of their subject. As the years went by I became better at it and my marks improved accordingly.

The only time I came seriously unstuck with this method was in the fourth year psychology exam - a half-day (or was it a whole-day) devoted to answering one question. There were always a number of questions to chose from but they all amounted to the same thing: "Evaluate everything you know about psychology". In my year there was a slight departure and one of the choices was "Evaluate everything you know about measurement theory as it applies to psychology". I was fascinated by measurement theory and knew an enormous amount about it so of course chose that question for my marathon answer. When time was up after several hours I had only just finished writing my neat summary – filling several exam books.

This presented my examiners with a dilemma – a circumstance I had previously carefully avoided. I obviously knew a great deal about the subject, but did a comprehensive dot-point summary really cut the ice in an essay exam? In the end they must have given me the benefit of the doubt because I passed the year and got into the PhD program. It taught me a valuable lesson – it is a good idea to leave enough time to rework what you have to offer into what the reader is looking for.

Early in my first year I was faced with another problem in presentation – how to present assignments. For the first time I was in a position where assignments were marked as part of an ongoing assessment. In those days before computers and word processors when only secretaries and professional writers had typewriters (or even knew how to operate them) most things were hand written, and for me this meant mostly unintelligible.

After my first psychology assignment – an experimental write-up that I had taken considerable effort and time to write neatly – Libby Delacy, the first year tutor, called me in for a chat and kindly suggested that I would get better marks if I bought myself a typewriter.

This I did and I typed every assignment from then on. I was still very prone to making mistakes but I quickly found that typescript is much easier to proofread and correct than handwriting. So with the help of a dictionary and whiteout I spent long hours improving my presentation. I subsequently gained the reputation of applying whiteout to my assignments rather extravagantly. Someone even suggested that my assignments looked like heavily applied makeup. Nonetheless after hours of typing and retyping on a long suffering second hand Remington I managed to produce assignments that were at least readable.

Fortunately I did not have any trouble with verbal presentations – except the usual stage fright that most students endure when presenting tutorials. I have had *the gift of the gab* from a very early age and soon learned not to bore people by reading my presentation from a prepared script. Of course I did prepare a script – sometimes that was also marked – but I then adapted my exam preparation technique and summarised my script so that I could present a 20-minute tutorial from a few words printed on a five by three card.

I maintained this system for the rest of my career and presented lectures, conference papers and workshops the same way. Eventually I could present a two-day workshop from half a dozen little cards. When PowerPoint came along towards the end of the nineties it was a small job to transfer my method from five by three cards to PowerPoint slides.

The problem with writing and spelling continues, but inconveniences me less and less. This is partly because I continue to put effort into learning correct spelling and partly because improvements in technology have made handwriting and spelling skills somewhat obsolete.

My biggest breakthrough came when I was 25 sitting at my desk writing up a section of my PhD thesis. It occurred to me that I could spell psychology and even epidiascope but I was sitting there puzzling over how many f's there were in *of* (or was it *off*). It struck me that spellings I had learned as an adult were easier for me than those I had learned as a child. Could it be that my brain had matured sufficiently to "get" spelling? From that moment I set about learning the simple spellings that had previously puzzled me. Whenever I came across a word that I was unsure of I would ask someone how to spell it and write it down on my by then ubiquitous five by three cards. These I would take out of my shirt pocket and rehearse at odd moments in the day until I was sure I was remembering them correctly.

I continue this process to this day albeit somewhat less zealously. I am currently working through the more arcane rules and exceptions surrounding doubling of letters. I'm also trying to track down why it would be that the word *until* ends in a single 'l' whereas its shortened form *till* ends in two. If you have the answer to this question or any examples of the same principle by all means send me an email to ianhills@antmail.com.au.

Keeping my spelling accurate is made more complex by the subtle changes that occur in spelling over time and geographical location. For example in traditional English spelling it is usual to use the letter 'z' as in 'organize' and the vowel combination 'ou' as in colour', whereas in America the usual spelling is the letter 's' and the vowel 'o' as in 'organise' and 'color'. Over the last 50 years as Australia's political and economic affiliations have shifted from England to America our spelling has followed suit. Learning to spell has thus become a continuous process in this country. So I continue to learn to spell as we all do.

A second major breakthrough for me came with the advent of word processors with spellchecking. I was an early adopter of these advances in IT, so early in fact that my first word processor ran on DOS (a pre windows Microsoft operating system) and would only write in capital letters. The computer was a TRS80 also known as *Trash 80* and the word processor didn't have a spellcheck, but did have the advantage that I could make corrections without the use of copious amounts of whiteout.

My current word processor by comparison not only writes in both upper and lower case but will also correct my spelling mistakes without asking. My current writing is both legible and properly spelled (or spelt if you are reading this in England). On the other hand when I proofread I have to watch out for words that my word processor thinks I meant which in fact I didn't.

It's been a long journey from the university student who struggled with written presentation. My presentation has improved through the thousands of exams, assignments, reports and papers I have written during my career and now I'm a retired psychologist writing my memoirs. No doubt if you read closely you will see signs of that journey and if you read closely enough no doubt you will pick up some spelling errors. If you do by all means send me a comment so that I can make the appropriate corrections. I'm still learning.

Link
Send comments to ianhills@antmail.com.au

CHAPTER 11

Learning my trade

I learned the basics of psychology in my first year (and passed the exams), but so much of it melded with all the other new information I was absorbing that I didn't get a clear idea of psychology as a subject until second year.

In second year I was able to do two psychology subjects, IIA: the theoretical strand consisting of the core subjects of psychology, and IIB: the practical strand which consisted mainly of social and industrial (now more commonly called *organisational*) psychology.

I can still recall some of the lectures and practicals but my clearest memory is of the environment in which we learned. The new Social Sciences building was still under construction and there was a general shortage of classrooms at the university campus so most of our lectures and practical sessions were held at the old university campus in George St, tucked away in Brisbane's Botanical Gardens.

There were some rather nice buildings in the complex, including the old Queensland parliament, but our classrooms were in the section that looked as if it was once an army training area. The Nissan huts were in considerable disrepair and quite dirty. Of especial note was the male toilet, which had a long section of windows (once opaque) at shoulder height above the urinal. At some point in our second year these were vandalised to the point where, as one student expressed it, you could *look before you leak.* The windows were never repaired as far as I know and soon after we completed our third year the buildings were condemned and later demolished. Classes and research still continued at George St until 1972, but psychology moved most of its activities to the new social sciences building around 1964.

Ironically, as part of the instruction in industrial psychology, we learned about the effect of the physical environment on performance in these drab, unedifying, dilapidated structures. Neither the students nor the lecturers showed any sign that there was a contradiction between what we were learning (that performance is better in more attractive surroundings) and what we were experiencing (being expected to perform in unattractive surroundings) . Later we received instruction on how people handle cognitive dissonance – which occurs when a person tries to reconcile contradictory ideas.

Another great example of the non-application of industrial psychology principles to our environment was the plumbing in the staffroom in the brand new social sciences building. At some point someone decided that it would be a good idea to install a tea urn next to the sink. Possibly for neatness' sake the tap for the boiling water was placed between the existing hot and cold taps. This resulted in the outlet for the boiling water being located just above the boiling water tap. It was impossible to turn on the tap without placing your hand directly in the path of a stream of boiling water. I never heard anyone comment on this devilish arrangement or on the consummate skill required to turn on the tap and withdraw the hand fast enough to avoid being scalded. Yet everyone learned how to do it – after the first time.

These days *workplace health and safety* would have taken care of this hazard in a jiffy. In the sixties you were just grateful for boiling water on tap and got on with making a cuppa.

The drab internal environment of our classrooms at the old George St. campus contrasted with the magnificent external environment. The Brisbane Botanic Gardens were at our doorstep and at lunchtime we could picnic on the lawns and often did – as long as we remembered to bring our own sandwiches – it was a long walk to the nearest shop.

I had many enjoyable lunchtimes on those lawns, including one memorable one in which I received a long lecture on the merits of confining one's sexual activity to one's own social class from a fellow (female) student. She used the word *slumming* to indicate her disapproval. I didn't know quite what to make of it – except that my fellow students probably knew that my girlfriend was not attending university. Was this young woman coming on to me or simply letting a social reprobate know what the rules were?

In retrospect I was shocked on two levels – firstly the implication that dating was linked to social class or possibly IQ. Secondly that sex was being openly discussed at all. This was my first inkling that the sexual revolution was on its way – or had perhaps already passed overhead without my noticing.

Among the practical skills we learned at the George St campus was how to train a rat in a Skinner box to bang a bar to get food pellets. Even though Skinner was able to demonstrate basic laws of learning with these clever little boxes (and not so clever rats) it is actually quite hard to get the rats to do what Skinner says they do. They will of course demonstrate quite clearly that a rat is more likely to bang a bar if you give it a food pellet straight away every time it does it. But how do you persuade the rat to hit the bar in the first place? This is the bit that Skinner is somewhat vague on. He calls the process *shaping* and suggests that rewards can be used to *shape* the rat's behaviour progressively towards the desired outcome but he gives no practical hints.

In practice the shaping takes at least as long as any other part of the experiment. It means spending hours and days waiting for the rat to wander closer to the bar so that you can reward it with a food pellet; and then waiting till it put its paw on the bar; and then waiting till it actually pressed the bar. All the time hoping that you don't fall asleep and miss the crucial moment.

The best part of the whole exercise was the relationship I formed with the rat. He had a cheeky, inquisitive personality that produced the few highlights of the whole experience. A few years later I came across a cartoon in McConnell's journal, the Worm Runner's Digest that summed up the experience for me. In the cartoon two rats are in adjacent Skinner boxes. One rat is saying to the other something like *I've just about got this experimenter trained. I just bang this bar and he drops a pellet into the bowl. You should try it.*

Interestingly enough the long hours spent training my rat gave me some useful insights that came in handy in my later psychological practice. The idea that rats, pigeons, people – in fact all animals - respond well to encouragement, reward and praise is not new. Spending hours and days and weeks using that principle to communicate my wishes to a non-verbal animal has cemented that idea firmly into my brain. It became part of my behavioural repertoire to observe and respond second by second.

For example during the first month of my first clinical job in the late sixties I was asked to get a severely withdrawn middle-aged alcoholic to eat, talk, leave his bed and socialise with other patients in the ward. I started with eating. I smiled and paid attention when he was sipping his liquid supplement and ignored him completely when he wasn't drinking. After ten minutes he said "I know what you are trying to do," lifted his glass and sculled the lot. This was the first time he had eaten and the first words he had said since entering the ward. I beamed - a double success. Soon he was up and about and even walked to the canteen for breakfast the next day. This success improved my credibility on the ward enormously although the psychiatrist in charge declaimed rather imperiously that she had been sure that I would fail because she thought that the patient wasn't intelligent enough to benefit from behaviour therapy. I refrained from informing her that I had honed my skills on rats.

I'm not sure if influencing our behaviour was an intended consequence of making second year psychology students spend so many hours communicating with rats, but I rather suspect it was.

We also learned to communicate with humans in a series of experiments exploring organisational structure, leadership qualities, decision-making, conformity and other qualities of human interaction. It was a lot more interesting and fun that trying to communicate with rats but had similar real life impacts. We were learning about how people and groups behave and it provided some life changing experiences. Later when I was teaching psychology myself I used similar experimental and experiential activities to encourage my students to gain insight into themselves and others as psychologists and people.

Gordon Mangan and John Damm, two very different lecturers, conducted these practical sessions and much of the lecturing in second year. Dr Mangan was a tall man. He dressed well but untidily like an English absent-minded professor. He always wore a bow tie, spoke precisely in a posh accent and gave an overall impression that he was somewhat eccentric. John Damm on the other hand was stocky, bearded and Aussie through and through. He dressed like an upmarket jackeroo and had a great sense of humour. Between them they ran an interesting series of lectures and practicals.

A good example of their approach was an experiment, that I feel sure was published later, to demonstrate the effect of physiological arousal on visual acuity. For this exercise half the class fasted until the afternoon prac class. We all then attempted to detect the first glimmer of light from a stimulus box, as it was gradually intensified. The hungry students quite clearly detected the light well before the ones who had eaten. I think even the lecturers were impressed.

Mangan's lectures on the nervous system were memorable – although I remember being quite confused with the details of different parts of a rat's brain. It took me a long time to learn what all the bits were called. These lectures and the clinical course run the following year by Elsie Harwood provided the basis for some of my later clinical work in the diagnosis of brain dysfunction.

Fortunately I found the human brain easier to understand, possibly because I had spent so much time trying to understand the rat brain.

Links
Worm Runner's Digest
http://en.wikipedia.org/wiki/Worm_Runner's_Digest
Skinner
http://www.simplypsychology.org/operant-conditioning.html

CHAPTER 12

Dr Gordon Mangan

Dr Mangan was far more influential in my development as a psychologist than I realised when I was a student. I must confess that I didn't warm to him as a teacher. When I peruse his publications it seems amazing that I can't find a full biography or bibliography of Mangan anywhere on the net. I am happy to fill that gap now. It is high time.

Dr Mangan has a rare scientific talent that enables him to originate and follow uncommon ideas to their conclusion and then substantiate his remarkable ideas with clear theorising and hard experimental data.

An overview of his publications might lead to the impression that he deliberately chose areas that were neglected and controversial. He devoted half a decade of his early career to parapsychology, publishing innovative research and clearheaded reviews. He devoted the latter part of his career to research in smoking – funded by the tobacco industry.

He had a lasting interest in Russian psychology particularly Pavlov and the neo-Pavlovians. A considerable amount of his work is devoted to drawing parallels between Eastern and Western conceptualisations of personality, learning and arousal which culminated in an influential book *The Biology of Human Conduct: East-West Models of Temperament and Personality*.

As well as these three areas he published on a broad range of topics including intelligence, aging, learning, conflict, behaviour therapy, personality, attention, music and arousal.

The following outline is a condensation that does not do justice to the innovation and complexity of his thinking nor to his adventurous approach to psychology. I feel privileged to have been taught by him and I like to think that some of my own adventurous approach to psychology is due in part to his influence.

Dr Gordon Mangan was born in New Zealand in 1924 and completed his schooling there before taking the entrance examination to enter the University of Aukland. In 1945 he was awarded a Masters degree in Education for his thesis involving a partial norming survey of the Stanford-Binet intelligence test of 15 and 16 year olds in New Zealand.

Subsequently he moved to Melbourne where in 1952 he obtained a Bachelor of Education degree at the University of Melbourne. Following this he obtained a place in the PhD program at the University of London and was awarded a PhD in 1954.

After a short stint as a high school teacher in 1954 he obtained a joint appointment as fellow of the Parapsychology Foundation and research associate at Duke University. In the fifties and sixties the Parapsychology Foundation and Duke University were renowned for taking the lead in research in paranormal psychology such as extra sensory perception (ESP) and psychokinesis (PK). In the following five years Dr Mangan made a substantial contribution to the parapsychology literature, publishing four experimental studies and three reviews.

In 1956 Dr Mangan joined the Department of Psychology at Queen's University in Canada and in 1958 he taught at the Psychology Department of Victoria University in Canada during which time he continued to publish in parapsychology and other areas such as personality and aging.

After that productive five years of parapsychology research, Dr Mangan never published in the area again but he carried his experience in the area with him to the University of Queensland in 1961. It was most likely his influence that induced me to risk my reputation on an experiment examining ESP in ants. It was a disaster that is fully reported in Chapter 19 *Ants and the death wish.*

The only conclusion that I could draw from that experiment was either ants have ESP and a very powerful death wish, or I had overlooked a very important variable: probably the latter. I did not mention the experiment to anyone for many years.

I attended Dr Mangan's classes during his time as Senior Lecturer in Psychology at University of Queensland. He gave many of the second and third year lectures in learning theory, social psychology, neurology and psychophysics and conducted many of the practical sessions as well.

Towards the end of his time at Queensland University Dr Mangan published prodigiously – more than a dozen papers in two years – on topics as diverse as personality variables related to visual sensitivity and the orienting reaction, arousability and distraction, after-images and personality, and approach-avoidance conflict. He ran and published a Behaviour Therapy Symposium and began publishing in the field that was to become a major research area for him – the relationship between Pavlovian (Russian) and Eysenckian (Western) personality paradigms.

Soviet psychology generated a lot of interest in the University of Queensland Psychology Department, as in many others in the Western world and Dr Mangan led enthusiastic discussion of Pavlov's dog experiments and Pavlov's typology.

Strangely this enthusiasm did not extend to replicating Pavlov's experiments and I don't recall much experimentation along these lines being conducted in Queensland at the time. This might be because some of Pavlov's experiments were considered cruel, or possibly because a publication citing Russian authors might attract the attention of ASIO – Australia's security service. Even in the late sixties it was still a bad career move in Australia to be associated in any way with communism.

Even so a small but brave contingent from the Queensland University Psychology Department made a scientific visit to Russia in the sixties and presumably had to put up with the attentions of ASIO. I might add that Dr Mangan who led this expedition moved to England shortly thereafter where he could enjoy a more tolerant politico-academic environment.

Dr Mangan continued his interest in Russian psychology and twenty years later wrote an influential book integrating Russian and Western personality theories. Even in the sixties at Queensland University he had developed the basics of his theory and I recall him discussing the similarity between extraversion-introversion (from the Western paradigm) and excitation-inhibition (from the Russian paradigm). Similarly he drew a parallel between the neuroticism dimension (after Catell and Eysenck) and Pavlov's strong-weak nervous system dichotomy.

After leaving Queensland University in the mid-seventies Dr Mangan joined one of England's elite Universities and taught psychology at Oxford. While at Oxford he continued to explore the similarities between Eastern and Western Psychology and published papers outlining the genetic, personality and nervous system implications.

While at Oxford in 1982 he published his best-known work "**The Biology of Human Conduct: East-West Models of Temperament and Personality**". He also published in other areas, for example papers on repression and muscle tension and the genetics of the nervous system.

While at Oxford Dr Mangan controversially tapped a rich vein of research funding from the tobacco industry and began a long association with the industry with publications on smoking maintenance, smoking and learning and the psychopharmacology of smoking.

According to Adams (2016) by 1981, some time after arriving at Oxford, Mangan began talking about returning to New Zealand and after a few years he moved to the University of Aukland where he stayed until his retirement.

During a decade in Aukland at the end of his career Dr Mangan continued to research at a lively pace, publishing papers on **personality and conditioning, music and IQ, IQ and reaction time, IQ and Evoked Potential, smoking and IQ,** and on reaction time and memory. He also revised and published a further edition of "The Biology of Human Conduct".

After a long, productive and interesting career as a researcher and teacher of psychology Dr Mangan continued to publish innovative research until 1995 when he was 72.

His latest publication is a further reprinting of *The Biology of Human Conduct* published in 2013 when Dr Mangan was 89 years old.

In 2016 a Google search for *Is Gordon Lavelle Mangan still alive in New Zealand?* yields a typically dry-wit Mangan response of *He most certainly is :).* He was then 92 years old.

Bibliography

A full Mangan bibliography appears in the Appendix.

Adams, P. J. (2016). *Moral Jeopardy: Risks of Accepting Money from the Alcohol, Tobacco and Gambling industries*. Cambridge, UK: Cambridge University Press.

Hills, I. M. (2016). Dr Gordon Lavelle Mangan (1924 -): A biographical note. *My alternative Wikipedia*. Retrieved from http://jrwik.blogspot.com.au/2016/07/gordon-lavelle-mangan-1924-biographical.html

Hills, I. M., Dr Gordon Lavelle Mangan, 2016, *Wikipedia*. Retrieved from https://en.wikipedia.org/wiki/Dr_Gordon_Lavelle_Mangan

Kiwi, The Annual Magazine Of The Students' Association, (1945). Auckland University College 1945

Mangan, Gordon Lavelle (1924-). *Encyclopedia of Occultism and Parapsychology.* (2001). Retrieved from
http://www.encyclopedia.com/doc/1G2-3403802939.html

Links
Mangan Publication timeline
http://www.worldcat.org/identities/lccn-n82-119175/

University of Melbourne Degrees Conferred 1952 at: https://digitised-collections.unimelb.edu.au/bitstream/handle/11343/23444/110442_UMC 195314_Degrees%20Conferred%201952.pdf?sequence=15

Is Gordon Mangan still alive?
http://www.answers.com/Q/Is_Gordon_lavelle_mangan_still_alive_in_New_Zealand

CHAPTER 13

Human beings and other animals

The psychology department was becoming quite interested in animal behaviour in the early sixties and even had a visiting lecturer whose speciality it was. His office door was adorned with a cartoon of him speaking wisely on the phone with a surprised looking pig.

The behaviour of animals was a big discussion point in my second and third year and of course parallels were drawn with human behaviour. We were often warned not to anthropomorphise especially in the area of emotions.

I found this a little strange. True we were starting to accept that human beings are animals, but apparently we were very special animals and this specialness set us clearly apart. Just because some animals behave like us, we were told, doesn't mean they are like us. In particular animals are not supposed to have emotions. A gorilla in a zoo shouldn't be called depressed even if he does spend all day sitting huddled in a corner and if he spends all day masturbating it would not be true to say he is emotionally disturbed.

Distinctions drawn between animals and humans included human's use of speech and tools. Even in those far off days I wondered about talking parrots, birdsong, dog barks, whale song, apes using twigs to pick insects from their holes and the otter's clever use of a stone to break open molluscs; and I wondered if the distinction between humans and other animals was a bit artificial. Was it possible that this distinction was being proposed only to bolster our sense of self-importance? Or worse was it a modern version of Genesis 1:26, framed so that we may continue to have *dominion over the fish of the sea and over the birds of the heavens and over the livestock?*

A really important distinction between people and animals we were told was that people don't have instincts. The range of complex *wired in* responses of animals fascinated me. Lorenz arranged to be the first animal seen by hatching ducklings and was imprinted as their mother. Mud dauber wasps will place their catch an exact distance from the mud nest and enter the nest before depositing the catch in it. Every time. If you continually move the catch while the wasp is in the nest it will doggedly deposit the catch at exactly the right spot and renter the nest without its catch again and again.

The full range of instincts includes behaviours associated with mating, feeding and raising young, communicating, dominance and a host of others.

Of course animals can learn new patterns of behaviour but, we were told, humans are unique in learning all our behaviour and having no inflexible instinctive behaviours. This did not seem right to me. Surely if we are part of the animal kingdom we would share this basic survival tactic – to pass on instinctive survival behaviours to our offspring without their having to learn them.

I was so interested in this apparent paradox that I decided to title my first tutorial presentation *Human Instinct*. I prepared thoroughly and was gratified with a good turnout – even some lecturers showed up. I put the argument that what we classify as reflexes seem very close to instincts in the way they operate. For example a baby doesn't usually have to learn to suck a nipple – it just knows to do it from the first.

I went on to note that humans have behaviour patterns that parallel the instinctive behaviour of animals in similar situations. For example many animals have an instinct called *imprinting* which occurs between parent and offspring and creates a complex of behaviours that assist in the survival of the young. Surely, I argued, there is a strong parallel between this and the human mother-child bond called *attachment* which is considered so important to normal human development. I argued that if *imprinting* is an instinctive behaviour pattern then *attachment* should properly be considered as instinctive too.

A similar behaviour pattern called *pair bonding* occurs between mating couples in the animal kingdom. It involves a complex of behaviours such as attachment to and protection of the mate, nest building, hatching and feeding that assist in the safe production of young. I argued that this behaviour pattern is so similar to the human experience of *falling in love* (attachment to the mate, house building, production of young) that they could be considered as examples of the same phenomenon. So I suggested that if *pair bonding* is an instinctive behaviour pattern then *falling in love* should properly be considered as instinctive too.

In the early sixties these arguments were considered heretical by behaviourist psychologists of that time. Unsurprisingly therefore this tutorial resulted in my being marked out as a student to be kept an eye on – either as a promising young student or as a loose cannon or possibly both. I was of course blissfully unaware of this until many years later.

Things have moved on and if I were giving a tutorial on human instincts today there is plenty of new material I could call on and my ideas have developed as well.

These days the idea that people might have instincts is less unorthodox. The writings of people like Richard Dawkins (The Selfish Gene, 1976), Steven Pinker (The Language Instinct, 1994) and Robert Winston (Human Instinct, 2002) have introduced the idea of human instincts to the scientific community and the broader public. Recently there has been some interesting research, which supports the idea of human instincts, for example Hanna Aronsson's 2011 PhD thesis *On Sexual Imprinting in Humans.*

It is interesting that these exciting thinkers and researchers include only one psychologist – Steven Pinker. The others are a zoologist, a biologist and a medical scientist. This distribution of talent seems to be representative of the field and is indicative of the difficulty that psychology as a discipline still has with the notion of human instinct. Within psychology Pinker's writing on instinct is considered controversial. Within zoology, and biology the idea of human instinct hardly raises an eyebrow.

The reasons why psychology continues to turn away from the idea of instinct are hard to discern. It might have something to do with the doctrine that all human behaviour is the result of learning. But to my mind it seems odd to acknowledge instinct in all other animal species but deny it in our own.

The reluctance to accept the idea of human instinct may be connected to the notion that instinctive behaviour is considered to be fixed and unchanging from one generation to the next. This view however is somewhat limited. Even the readiness of ducklings to imprint at a certain age has a considerable degree of flexibility. Lorenz clearly showed that while imprinting is more or less inevitable for ducklings the focus of imprinting is not fixed. It doesn't have to be the genetic parent duck, or even another duck that ducklings imprint on. It doesn't even have to be an animal. Some of Lorenz' ducklings imprinted on a beach ball!

Complicating the picture further is the possibility that some human instincts may conflict with each other. For example the selfish gene described by Dawkins may clash with an altruism gene – a set of behaviours designed to promote the interests of the group and equally likely to have evolved as survival behaviour. It seems possible that what we call ethics may in fact be the way in which each of us finds our individual way of resolving these conflicting behaviour patterns.

It might even be suggested that sexual morality may result from the resolution on two conflicting patterns of sexual behaviour present in most humans. The monogamous sexual pattern has good value for the survival of our genes in that it ensures that our offspring have a better start in life. The promiscuous sexual pattern also has good value for the survival of our genes in that it is likely to produce more offspring for men and allows women to choose the most viable father for their children.

Humans seem to engage in both patterns, sometimes at the same time, and our judgement of sexual morals seem bound up in the way individuals resolve the conflicting demands of these two behaviour patterns.

These examples are only two of the ways in which human instincts could result in a wide variety of behaviour.

Many psychologists on the other hand view the idea of human instincts as seriously deterministic. Psychology as a discipline seems to have missed the point that human behaviour can still be gloriously variable even if some of it is instinctive.

This is a pity and not only because psychology is denying itself an interesting and useful field of study. I think it likely that the perspective that psychology can bring to bear would result in a far richer understanding of the interplay between human instinct and learning than currently exists.

It is also possible that I'm still regarded as a loose cannon.

Bibliography

Aronsson, H. (2011). *On Sexual Imprinting in Humans* (Unpublished PhD thesis). Stockholm University.

Beach, F. A. (1955). The descent of instinct. *Psychological Review*, 62(6), 401-410.

Birney, R. C. & Teevan R. C. (1961). *Instinct: an enduring problem in psychology.* NY: Van Nostrand.

Dawkins, R. (1976). *The Selfish Gene.* Oxford University Press

Denton, D. A. (1982). *The Hunger for Salt: An Anthropological, Physiological and Medical Analysis. Heidelberg: Springer Verlag.*

Pinker, S. (1994). *The Language Instinct* . New York, NY: Harper Perennial Modern Classics.

Winston, R. (2002). *Human Instinct.* London: Bantam Press

Links

Human Bonding
http://en.wikipedia.org/wiki/Human_bonding

Imprinting
http://en.wikipedia.org/wiki/Imprinting_(psychology)

Pair bonding
http://en.wikipedia.org/wiki/Pair_bond

Steven Pinker
http://en.wikipedia.org/wiki/Steven_Pinker

Robert Winston
http://en.wikipedia.org/wiki/Robert_Winston

CHAPTER 14

Is there such a thing as human instinct?

For around 60 years psychologists have maintained that humans do not have instincts – that all our behaviour is learned. Recently scientists from other disciplines have questioned this view and proposed that many of our behaviour patterns are inherited. It has even been suggested that psychologists' rejection of instinct is based on ideology rather than science – that we could not bring ourselves to believe that human beings are programmed by genetics.

Back in the 60s when I first started thinking about this issue I did not have any well formed ideas about what instinct was and my thinking didn't get much beyond *the emperor's got no clothes* idea that the current theoretical position in psychology had huge logical problems.

Whether or not humans have instincts rests entirely on how instinct is defined. The definition that we have endorsed for the last 60 years has major problems. I suspect that this definition devised in 1960 by Beach (1955), formalised by Birney and Teevan (1961) and endorsed by their colleagues, may have been deliberately framed to exclude human behaviour because the idea that human behaviour may be programmed by DNA was unpalatable to them. In the sixties psychologists regarded as a heresy the idea that anything other than learning theory applied to human behaviour. Psychology has grown up a bit since then. For example we now acknowledge that thinking is a behaviour we can study whereas previously it was held that the mind was a *black box* and thoughts were unknowable. Perhaps we have developed enough that we can now also admit to inherited behaviour.

I think Beach and his colleagues went too far. Beach wrote that he hoped that with further work he could make the concept of instinct disappear and be replaced by a more scientific explanation (Beach, 1955). The definition of instinct they framed was so prescriptive that almost no behaviour, animal or human, could be described as instinctive. Or alternatively all behaviour could be described as instinctive by this definition, courtesy of the innocuous seeming rider at the end of the definition.

Beach's colleagues set out 5 characteristics of instincts in *Instinct: an enduring problem in psychology* (Birney and Teevan, 1961) all of which had to be present for a behaviour to be termed instinctive. Instinct had to:

a) be automatic,
b) be irresistible,
c) occur at some point in development,
d) be triggered by some event in the environment,
e) occur in every member of the species,
f) be unmodifiable, and
g) govern behaviour for which the organism needs no training   (although the organism may profit from experience and to that degree the behaviour is modifiable).

It seems to me that a), b) and f) suggest the behaviour has no flexibility but even a cursory observation of animals will reveal that considerable flexibility occurs in instinctive behaviour. Some hens have a stronger mothering instinct and some bulls are much more versed in sexual behaviour than others. Young bulls tend to ride each other as a sort of practice run, but their mating behaviour is considered instinctive. Lorenzo's ducks were not all that choosy about what they imprinted on - they had considerable flexibility in the choice of *mother object* so f) does not seem to apply to them. Spiders sent into space lose their ability to make well-organised webs, so f) does not appear to apply to them either.

c) suggests *a moment in time* can be attached to instinctive behaviour but this does not seem to be the case. Birds build nests, pair bond and migrate year after year for many years.

e) suggests that finding a member of a species that does not exhibit a designated behaviour would disqualify that behaviour from being an instinct. As against this, we know that all characteristics are expressed on a bell shaped curve and at one extreme the possibility of non-occurrence exists. In practical terms, birds that do not pair bond have been noted, some migrating birds are left behind and die each season and some bulls just don't seem to get the hang of mating; and yet these behaviours are all described as instinctive.

The rider in g) which allows instinctive behaviour to profit from experience seems to run counter to most of the rest of the definition. Applying it would allow almost any behaviour to be described as instinctive.

These are just some of the problems I see with the Birney and Teevan definition of instinct. The main problem is that the definition we have been working from all these years was framed by a group of people who didn't like the idea of instinctive behaviour and hoped they could make it disappear by defining it out of existence. It's time to re-examine the definition and try for something more useful. I think that Beach might perhaps agree with me, if he were still alive. He once suggested that science should be published in ink that faded after 10 years, so that previous theories would not hinder progress.

My working definition of instinct for the moment is *inherited behaviour*. I like to keep it simple.

Other writers have had a go at modifying the definition of instinct to accommodate more recent data and the possibility of the existence of instinct in humans. For example Denton (1982) proposed an inherited *trinity neural organisation* involving sensory inflow components, compelling intention, and emotion.

Rourke (2013) suggests *genetically transmitted knowledge that leads to behaviour common to a particular species* as a definition of instinct and describes four types: unthinking skill (e.g. the ability to fly), innate urge (e.g. to migrate at a certain time of year), possession of knowledge (e.g. knowing where to go), and ability to (genetically) pass the knowledge on to the next generation. He also proposes that instinctive does not necessarily imply unthinking and describes instinctive behaviours that would require some cognitive processing to be successful - such as ability to apply knowledge of a migration route in order to fly along it.

Other writers such as Richard Dawkins (The Selfish Gene, 1976), Steven Pinker (The Language Instinct, 1994) and Robert Winston (Human Instinct, 2003) have used broader definitions of instinct that include human behaviours.

I would throw into the argument:

1. The interaction between instinctive behaviour and environmental influences has been neglected. If genetic inheritance of disease proneness can be influenced by environmental influences such as diet and pollution then it would be logical to suppose that inherited behaviour could interact in quite complex ways with environmental factors and produce a great variety in the expression of instinctive behaviours.

2. Human instincts can conflict with each other, producing flexibility. The idea of instinctive behaviour being *robotic* in character is to my mind a gross oversimplification and has been a major factor in leading psychologists to unnecessarily reject the idea of human instinct.

3. DNA transmission of survival behaviour is such a powerful survival technique that it doesn't seem possible for us to have become the most successful species on the planet without it.

4. We share high percentage of our genes with our closest relatives - the apes. Apes have instincts. If we do not, then all the instinctive behaviour of apes must be packed into a tiny amount of genetic material. This doesn't seem very likely to me. I think instinctive behaviour would take up a lot of gene space.

5. Humans have imprinting and pair bonding behaviours. We call them attachment and falling in love. In other animals we call them instincts so we should in humans.

6. Humans have complex reflexes (e.g. infant breast feeding) that fit the Beach definition of instinct and differ from other instincts only in degree of complexity. I think the distinction is arbitrary and so-called reflexes could be redefined as instinctive

We do need a better definition of instinct. The definition by Beach and his colleagues has unfortunately resulted in psychology as a profession ignoring this area and leaving all the interesting innovations to biologists, zoologists, medical scientists among others. The unique perspective of psychology has been almost absent from this interesting area for around 60 years. I hope this will change soon.

Bibliography

Aronsson, Hanna. (2011). *On Sexual Imprinting in Humans* (Unpublished PhD thesis). Stockholm University, Department of Zoology.

Beach, F. A. (1955). The descent of instinct. *Psychological Review*, 62(6), 401-410.

Birney, Robert C. & Teevan Richard C. (1961). *Instinct: an enduring problem in psychology*. New York: Van Nostrand.

Dawkins, Richard. (1976). *The Selfish Gene*. New York: Oxford University Press.

Denton, D.A. (1982). *The Hunger for Salt: An Anthropological, Physiological and Medical Analysis*. Heidelberg: Springer Verlag.

Pinker, Steven. (1994). *The Language Instinct: How the Mind Creates Language*. New York, NY: Harper Perennial Modern Classics.

Rourke, B. (2013). *The origins of human behaviour*. Houston Tx: Strategic Book Publishing and Rights Co.

Winston, Robert. (2003). *Human Instinct*. London: Bantam Press

CHAPTER 15

Culture and family

As well as two subjects in Psychology my second year studies included first year Anthropology, a subject that fascinated me, and second year French in which I thought I could coast. I thought my long association with French during my English schooling and holidays in France would carry me through yet another year of French study without much effort. It didn't and I failed French ll. Even so I have had the opportunity to use my schoolboy French on several occasions since, although I must confess I haven't put much effort into maintaining my ability to speak and write French.

Anthropology was quite a different matter and sparked my interest immediately. Having lived for short periods in countries other than my own as a child I had a modest appreciation of different ways of life, but studying anthropology opened a vista of cultures that took my mental breath away and made me look at my own society through different eyes.

We studied ancient and modern cultures and a variety of techniques ranging from archaeology to ethnography, linguistic analysis to survey research. We studied different systems of economics, politics, kinship and religion.

I found it all fascinating and especially interesting when we applied these techniques to our own cultural environment. One exercise in particular had a profound effect on me. This exercise required each student to record a family tree from their own knowledge and compare it with a family tree constructed from the sum of knowledge within the family unit. My family unit contained my maternal grandmother who had detailed knowledge of our family going back several generations. As well as their relationship to us she also knew other things about them such as their current whereabouts, personality and occupation.

Like most families of my generation our family knowledge focussed mainly on our nuclear family unit and we had little knowledge outside that. With Nan's revelations I discovered that my family tree contained poets and authors, railway men and wheelwrights, soldiers and pacifists, suffragettes and indomitable Scots matriarchs, priests and nuns. I discovered that a big branch of our family originated in Kent and my father was born on a tiny island in the Hebrides called Rhum and his father died young during a bungled quinsy draining. To my surprise I found out that a branch of our family had migrated to Canada and I had a dozen cousins I hadn't known about.

Years later I discovered that some of this material was pure invention designed to conceal what Nan saw as the family's indiscretions. It was only to be expected I suppose.

The impact of this exercise was not only in the information Nan imparted just a few years before her death. I was also struck by the fact that it seemed to be accepted that in our society, in our time, family information is not usually passed on. I wonder if this is motivated by a sense that recent history has been deplorable and that the next generation is better off starting with a clean slate. This attitude is easy to understand and forgive in a family that had been through two world wars, the great depression, and other disasters and had decided to migrate to the other side of the world to start afresh.

The study of Anthropology has had a far-reaching effect on my career inclining me towards cross cultural research and practice. In the seventies I would teach a course in Anthropology at James Cook University, assist in the training of Aboriginal counsellors in Townsville and spend some time at Hawaii university studying and researching how to develop interculturally skilled counsellors. In the eighties I had a number of jobs that involved working with aborigines in remote, urban and educational settings.

Considering that my undergraduate anthropology courses were taught in a country that is home to the Australian Aborigines – participants in the world's longest lasting distinctive cultures – it is surprising that so little of the coursework was devoted to the study of Aboriginal cultures. We learned about the focus on family and *skin* and the various artefacts used by Aboriginal people – boomerangs, spears, spear throwers, stone tools and coolamons – but with little suggestion that these ways of life are current and the artefacts currently in use. The information was presented with no more immediacy than if we had been studying the Aztecs and with the common evasion *they used to* with no sense that *they still do* and the environment in which they still do these things was all around us. Nobody suggested that we should invite representatives of those cultures, living close by, to come and teach us about their way of life. Things have changed a lot since then at least on the surface.

I realised later that this approach was entirely consistent with the standard approach to the Aboriginal population of Queensland at the time, that is: out of sight, out of mind. This is best exemplified by the fact that in the early sixties the state government had such tight control over the Aboriginal population that the majority of Aborigines were forcibly confined to settlements in the remoter areas of Queensland.

There were some exceptions and I met some of them during my second year at university. For example I spent some time with Oodgeroo Noonuccal, an Aboriginal poet then known by the name under which she published as Kath Walker. From her I began to understand some of the restrictions that Aborigines were struggling with. I had some classes in common with Margaret Valadian – the first Aborigine to study at Queensland University. We graduated in the same year: 1966.

These amazing women were part of a small and mostly invisible group of Aborigines who had been given exemption from the Act (the Queensland Aboriginals Preservation and Protection Acts, 1939 to 1946) and were allowed to live in any area of the state.

This contact with Aboriginal people has continued throughout the rest of my life and has led me to many interesting adventures, fascinating places and extraordinary people.

Links

Margaret Valadian
http://abceducation.net.au/videolibrary/view/margaret-valadian-82

Oodgeroo Noonuccal
http://en.wikipedia.org/wiki/Oodgeroo_Noonuccal

Kath Walker biography
http://www.biography.com/people/kath-walker-37858

CHAPTER 16

Culture, civil rights and song writing

In my undergraduate years I spent a fair amount of time writing songs with John Tomlinson who was instrumental in radicalising my thinking. John also introduced me to Oodgeroo Noonuccal, an Aboriginal poet then known by the name under which she published as Kath Walker.

We sat and chatted in Kath's tiny kitchen in an old Queenslander in Buranda, a downmarket suburb of Brisbane. I was struck by how familiar Kath's concerns were, and how very different.

Kath confided concerns about her health and her children. We had a long discussion about the best way to reduce prejudice against Aborigines and secure the human rights of Aboriginal people. Kath was in favour of constant small steps. John favoured a more radical approach. I found myself agreeing more with Kath.

We discussed poetry, Kath's, John's and mine and how hard it was to find a publisher who was willing to take the risk of publishing poetry. I forget the other subjects we discussed but the conversation went on for some time and ranged far and wide during which time Kath allowed me an insight into her world.

I came away with my first inkling of the restrictions that Aborigines were struggling with and the Aboriginal experience of living with two cultures, two ways of thinking and two laws. I'm not sure if it was Kath's deliberate intention to educate me in this way, but I am nonetheless conscious of a debt of gratitude to her for taking the trouble.

John Tomlinson was a committed supporter of the underdog and decidedly anti-authoritarian. Unlike many of our contemporaries John continued firm in his convictions throughout his life. Consistent with his beliefs he became a social worker and worked with the poor for most of his career. He wrote books that were influential in challenging and changing the practice of social work, he was a long time Director of the ACT Council of Social Service, and he taught at the Darwin Community College and the Queensland University of Technology.

John was involved in organising the folk music club at Queensland University in the early sixties but his interest was more in the influence of the words of folk songs than in the music. He persuaded me to put some of his radical poems to music and arranged venues for me to sing them. He enjoyed introducing me by claiming that we made a good song writing team because he was tone deaf and I was illiterate. I think (I hope) he meant dyslexic.

John actually was tone deaf – otherwise I'm sure he would have written his own music. As it was our composing sessions sometimes took on a pythonesque quality as I attempted to alter the structure of his poems to fit my music and he attempted to sing his version in a monotone guttural chant. As time went on I became adept at interpreting this deep guttural chant and my music was more in accord with his artistic vision.

In 1963 John arranged for me to sing at the Federal Council for the Advancement of Aborigines and Torres Strait Islanders conference in Canberra. We hitch-hiked there and back with my guitar and I sang a few sets of John's songs. At the conference I listened to a talk from an Aboriginal woman, Mrs Jean Jimmy, from Bamaga, one of the restricted settlements on Cape York. Mrs Jimmy had taken a great risk to leave without permission in order to tell the conference how the Mapoon people had been forcibly removed from their land and moved to Bamaga to make way for a bauxite mine.

I was deeply moved by Mrs Jimmy's description of the forcible evacuation and destruction of Mapoon and wrote a song very quickly in the break as she was chatting with the audience. I was able to hand the words of the song to her as she was being rushed from the conference room.

More than a year later I discovered that the song had been distributed through north Queensland and had eventually made its way to the Union Singers in Brisbane as they were looking for material to put on the flip side of their album *Ballad of Women*.

Margaret Kitamura had written new music for my song and the Union singers were told about my authorship of the lyrics by John who previewed the record just in time for my name to be included on the label.

I have heard the *folk process* defined as "what happens when two musicians forget different versions of the same folk song". I think the folk process probably improved my song – although I miss some of he bit that went missing in the year or so between when I wrote the song and Margaret recorded it. I titled the song *Black Friday*, because the Mapoon land clearance took place on a Friday the 13th and Mrs Jimmy called it *Black Friday*. I used the tag line

Whose Land as well as *Black Friday* as recurring refrains throughout the song. The folk process (and my poor handwriting) resulted in the title becoming *Whose Hand*, and the *Black Friday* tag disappearing altogether, along with a few other improvements to the lyrics.

It was my first music publication and a song I am still very proud of. It was subsequently recorded by Phil Lobl and of course myself. The soundtrack of my version of the song along with the words is at:

http://ianhillssongsandpoems.weebly.com/-whose-hand.html

John was very gracious about my success especially considering that he had put a lot of effort into scoring the FCAATSI gig to showcase his songs and the only lasting result turned out to be the success of one of mine.

Bibliography

Evans, R., Saunders, K. & Cronin, K. (1988). *Race Relations in Colonial Queensland: A History of Exclusion, Exploitation and Extermination.* St Lucia: University of Queensland Press.

Links

Ian Hills, Whose Hand
http://ianhillssongsandpoems.weebly.com/-whose-hand.html

Federal Council for the Advancement of Aborigines and Torres Strait Islanders
http://dictionaryofsydney.org/entry/federal_council_for_the_advancement_of_aborigines_and_torres_strait_islanders
http://indigenousrights.net.au/organisations/pagination/federal_council_for_the_advancement_of_aborigines_and_torres_strait_islanders_fcaatsi

Kath Walker biography
http://www.biography.com/people/kath-walker-37858
Oodgeroo Noonuccal
http://en.wikipedia.org/wiki/Oodgeroo_Noonuccal

Under the Act in Queensland
http://www.library.uq.edu.au/fryer/1967_referendum/act.html

Margaret Valadian
http://trove.nla.gov.au/people/636060?c=people
http://aiatsis.gov.au/bio/dr-margaret-valadian

Margaret Valadian, ABC Four Corners
http://abceducation.net.au/videolibrary/view/margaret-valadian-82

Whose Hand
Recorded in 1964 by Union Singers on LP 'The Ballad of Women" with music by Margaret Kitamura. http://unionsong.com/u501.html

Recorded in 1968 by Phil Lobl on LP 'Dark Eyed Daughter'
http://www.phyllobl.net/index.php?option=com_content&view=article&id=154:whose-hand&catid=58:dark-eyed-daughter&Itemid=130

Recorded in 1968 by Phil Vinnecombe on W&G 7" "Dark Eyed Daughter". https://www.discogs.com/Phyl-Vinnecombe-Dark-Eyed-Daughter/release/7327409

Recorded in 1983 by Ian Hills with original music by Ian Hills on cassette 'Chains Freedom and the Land'.

Available as a download 2013 from "Ian Hills Songs and Poems"
http://ianhillssongsandpoems.weebly.com/-whose-hand.html

CHAPTER 17

John Tomlinson: radical student

John Tomlinson and I were walking along a wide suburban street in Brisbane in the early nineteen sixties when we were students at Queensland University. It was a lovely spring day with the hot Queensland sun beating down. As we strolled along a street lined with high-set Queenslanders set on tiny bright green lawns, John was expounding with great emotion on the latest atrocities of the Queensland Government - the administration of Aboriginal Missions, the treatment of children in care, human rights abuses…the list was a long one. He was so angry, he was proposing that we line the politicians up against a wall and machine-gun them all for their crimes against humanity.

As we approached a little corner store there was a small child sitting on the curb crying. John stopped his tirade in mid sentence and sat on the curb next to the child. The little boy had dropped his sixpence down the drain and could not get it back. He'd had his heart set on buying an ice cream but now all he could do was to stare mournfully at the sixpence - in sight but out of reach in the drain. John and I tried unsuccessfully to get the sixpence out of the drain and then John took the child into the shop and bought him an ice cream.

The child sauntered off happily licking his ice cream. John continued his ferocious tirade against oppression as we walked on down the road.

There is something in that story that explains a lot about John: his support of the underdog, his abhorrence of oppression, his suspicion of authority, his hostility to abuse of power, and his practical compassion.

John and I met in the early sixties at a Student Action Group meeting called to set up a folk club at the University of Queensland. There was a long ideological discussion initiated by John about whether the offerings should be restricted to only radical modern folk songs. Almost everyone apart from John argued against such a left elitist approach. The folk club went ahead with an open agenda welcoming folk music of all kinds and was almost immediately immensely popular. Hundreds turned up to the Tuesday lunchtime concerts.

A year or so later the Folk Club came to an abrupt end when it was apparently thought to be a communist front organisation. Of course there had been plenty of leftist protest songs but plenty of traditional folk and love songs too. Nonetheless, the folk club was closed down, but the communists the club was supposedly fronting for were never identified. Undoubtedly some communists attended the lunchtime concerts – there were always some about at Universities – but I think calling the club a front was a bit of a stretch.

The communist menace was a great scare during the sixties, and to some a great joke. In Queensland the police Special Branch kept an eye on clubs and societies (especially University ones) to keep tabs on radicals, subversives and communists. I know of at least one student who made a habit of attending meetings and then reporting to special branch. In addition, a study-buddy of mine confided in me that she thought her boyfriend might be an ASIO spy and hinted that she had been asked to report on me.

I expect that John was of interest to Special Branch because of his political activities and his openly *fellow traveller* views. Neither of us was directly questioned as far as I know.

In the nineties the files of Special Branch were made available to their subjects prior to their purported destruction (of the files, not the subjects). People were invited to apply to look at their files. I decided not to, partly because I thought it would upset me and partly because I didn't trust the authorities not to use this exercise as a way of identifying people whom they should have been investigating but weren't yet.

As well as our shared interest in political activism John and I wrote protest songs and this took up a great deal of the time we spent together. I have written about our adventures with song writing in Chapter 16 *Culture, civil rights and song writing.* Many of our songs were about the problems facing Aborigines and the human rights abuses they suffered. After several years of collaboration we compiled a book of songs titled *Chains, freedom and the land.* I put a lot of work into laboriously writing out the musical scores and Aboriginal poet Kath Walker wrote a foreword to our book, but we weren't able to get a publisher and it languished unpublished in my filing cabinet for several years before I lost it in one of my many moves.

The first song of mine to be recorded on vinyl came about through my association with John. He arranged for me to sing some of his songs at the 1963 Federal Council for the Advancement of Aborigines and Torres Strait Islanders conference in Canberra. During the conference I wrote the song *Whose Hand* after I heard about the forcible removal of the Mapoon people from their land to make way for a bauxite mine. The song was distributed around north Queensland and was later picked up and recorded by the Union Singers on the B-side of their album *Ballad of Women*. John heard a preview of the record and was able to identify me as the author of *Whose hand* in time for the credits to include my name.

John introduced me to Kath Walker, the name under which Aboriginal poet Oodgeroo Noonuccal published in the 1960s. We sat and chatted in Kath's kitchen about poetry and publishers and the hard life of Aboriginal people. It was a startling educational experience for me on many levels.

Even before graduation John began his long career of outing oppression wherever he found it. He began by outing the Queensland Department of Children's Services, which had a reputation for unreasonably refusing to reunite children with their parents after the need for retaining the children in care had passed. He started a client organisation, which supported parents in conflict with the Department. His favourite joke of the time: *what's the difference between Children's Services and a Rottweiler? With a Rottweiler you eventually get your child back.*

John and I organised a visit to Aboriginal missions in north Queensland in the early sixties but at the last minute I was unable to go. John returned from that trip with ample evidence of human rights abuses on Aboriginal missions. He reported that the Queensland Aboriginal Protection Act was being given full effect: Aborigines were not allowed to move off settlements without permission; they were not allowed to own land; they were not allowed to marry without permission; their children were taken from them without cause, and many other restrictions and indignities. John railed against the practice of paying Aborigines with rations, usually strictly limited amounts of meat, sugar, flour and tea. He declaimed sarcastically that Aborigines on a particular mission in addition to their meagre rations were generously allowed to consume as much caster oil as they liked.

When he returned, John penned the lyrics to *Slave pay* which I put to music and sang whenever I had an audience. The chorus runs:

Slave pay, slave pay,
It's so low now.
I ain't complaining.
I ain't moaning.
I'm just saying
It's so low now.

Even after all these years that chorus has the power to send shivers down my spine and bring tears to my eyes.

Bibliography

Tomlinson, John. (1967). *Reflections of a fool.* Darwin: Wobbly Press.

Tomlinson, John. (1974). *Confessions of an opiate eater.* Darwin: Wobbly Press.

Tomlinson, John. (1977). *Is band-aid social work enough?* Darwin: Wobbly Press.

Tomlinson, John. (1982). *Social work community work.* Darwin: Wobbly Press.

Tomlinson, John. (1982). B*etrayed by bureaucracy.* Darwin: Wobbly Press.

Tomlinson, John. (1983). *The death of Phillip Robertson.* Darwin: Wobbly Press.

Tomlinson, John. (1999). *People's poems and songs of struggle.* Darwin: Wobbly Press.

Links

Special Branch
http://www.brisbanetimes.com.au/queensland/inside-queenslands-spy-unit-20100406-rpbg.html
https://woollydays.wordpress.com/2013/11/25/the-history-of-queenslands-special-branch-remembered/
https://griffithreview.com/articles/long-gone-but-not-forgotten/

Oodgeroo Noonuccal
http://en.wikipedia.org/wiki/Oodgeroo_Noonuccalhttp://www.biography.com/people/kath-walker-37858

Federal Council for the Advancement of Aborigines and Torres Strait Islanders

http://dictionaryofsydney.org/entry/federal_council_for_the_advancement_of_aborigines_and_torres_strait_islanders
http://indigenousrights.net.au/organisations/pagination/federal_council_for_the_advancement_of_aborigines_and_torres_strait_islanders_fcaatsi

Whose Hand
http://ianhillssongsandpoems.weebly.com/-whose-hand.html
http://rateyourmusic.com/release/album/various_artists_f2/ballad_of_women__whose_hand__and_other_songs.p/
http://trove.nla.gov.au/work/33805645?selectedversion=NBD22859868

CHAPTER 18

John Tomlinson: radical social worker

After John graduated in 1964 we lost touch for nearly 20 years. In that time John accomplished an amazing amount. He began his extensive publishing career in 1967 with a book of poetry *Reflections of a fool*. This was followed by another book of poetry *Confessions of an opiate eater* in 1974 and an influential book *Is band-aid social work enough?* in 1977. Subsequently he published *Social work community work* and *Betrayed by bureaucracy* in 1982, a play *The death of Phillip Robertson* in 1983 and a further book of poetry *People's poems and songs of struggle* in 1999. In addition he has other books and quite a swag of articles, scholarly essays and conference papers to his name.

When we met again in 1984 John had a lot to tell me. After working for a few years with the Northern Territory Welfare Branch he had returned to Brisbane to enrol in a Masters degree and in 1972 was awarded a Masters of Social Work for his work with Aborigines and Torres Strait Islanders in South Brisbane. His study demonstrated that Community Work methods involving close consultation with community groups had much better outcomes than the individual counselling approaches prevalent at the time.

In 1973 John returned to Darwin to work as Senior Social Worker in the Welfare Branch and was soon embroiled in controversy. Following discussions with other social workers he returned an Aboriginal child to its family against the wishes of a senior member of the Department. In the following inquiry it was determined that John had acted against instructions in reuniting the child with its family. On this basis he was given a punitive demotion to base level social worker. John relates how following his demotion to Grade 1, Les MacFarlane, the speaker of the Legislative Assembly, telegrammed the Department Can't you demote Tomlinson one more grade?

As a result of John's severe treatment over this issue the Social Workers of the Northern Territory Welfare Branch went on strike – the first social work strike in Australia.

For those interested in more detail John recently published an account of the incident in Yu and Mandell's book *Subversive action: extralegal practices for social justice* (Tomlinson, 2015).

Following John's example professionals in Australia could feel on more solid moral ground when defying authority to reunite Aboriginal children with their families. In Bundaberg in the nineties there were several occasions when I was in conflict with the Queensland Family Services Department over this issue and I took heart from John's example when pressing for action.

John's demotion had a very useful spin-off. He was sidelined with nothing to do, so he researched and wrote a very critical review of the emergency income support policies and practices of the Welfare Branch, which he gave a wide and high-level circulation. He was soon put back to work.

Soon after, at Christmas 1974, cyclone Tracy struck Darwin. I was Lecturing at James Cook University in Townsville at the time and volunteered with Life Line, which assisted the thousands of people who fled from Darwin through Townsville on their way to southern capitals. They were shell-shocked and destitute and desperate to get as far as they could from Darwin. One of the Engineers from James Cook University visited Darwin soon after the cyclone to examine the structural properties of buildings that had withstood the high winds. He returned with photographs of the devastation – demolished houses from horizon to horizon, unrecognisable streets, iron stobie poles bent parallel to the ground. He found only a handful of intact houses to examine.

When John and I met again in 1984 he talked of the hectic days following the cyclone. He had been in charge of issuing Emergency Purchase orders and of the Emergency Relief office at Casuarina High School. He remarked how much he had enjoyed giving away all the furniture belonging to the Welfare Branch to people who had lost everything in the cyclone.

After the cyclone John assisted in the reconstruction of Darwin as Social Planner with the Regional Council of Social Development. John recalls with satisfaction how, during a chance meeting at an official handover, he was instrumental in persuading the Clem Jones, the leader of the Darwin Reconstruction Commission, to demolish as unsafe the notorious juvenile prison, Essington House.

Later in the seventies John invited the police and the press to a screening of a video of alleged police brutality. After the screening the police produced a warrant, which John read and concluded that it was poorly prepared and probably invalid. He refused to give back until he had been given a copy. The ensuing struggle, as the police attempted to retrieve the warrant, was recorded by the press photographers and published in the following day's paper. The police had provided ample copy for a police brutality story.

One of the press photographs depicted John hunched over clutching the search warrant and large policemen attempting to wrest it from him. Later this photo appeared on the back of one of John's books captioned: *The author assisting the police with their enquiries.*

Later the Federal Court agreed that the warrant was insufficiently precise and the police had exceeded their powers. The charges against John were dropped.

During the East Timor conflict one of John's friends was arrested leaving Darwin harbour with a boatload of supplies allegedly destined for the Fretilin freedom movement. John had been asked to help by delivering the material to the harbor so the next day he was arrested too. One of the misdemeanours he was charged with was *aiding, abetting, counselling and being concerned with the illegal export of goods.* A friend quipped, It's about time a social worker was charged with counselling.

After a tiresome investigation the charges were dropped and the boat and the van were returned – albeit somewhat the worse for wear.

In 1977 John was appointed as Coordinator of the Community Work course at the Darwin Community College (later the Charles Darwin University) where he remained until 1985 when the course was discontinued.

During that time he published a small monthly magazine called *Farewell to Alms*. In John's words the magazine was devoted to having *the welfare system disassociate itself from the poor law charity system and embrace universal income guarantees such as a Guaranteed Minimum Income.* Trouble ensued when he wrote that the Director of NT Welfare was murdering Aboriginal children by restricting their parents' access to welfare. The Director brought charges of criminal libel against John for this statement. Thus, John became the first person to be charged with criminal libel following Frank Hardy's publication of *Power Without Glory* in 1950. John's legal advice was that he would lose the case and end up in jail so he reluctantly made an apology and retraction and later was sued in a civil libel case for a few thousand dollars.

He got his own back. In a later edition of *Farewell to Alms* he pointed out that by making it hard for parents to get welfare payments, the Director's actions were leading to the deaths of an increasing number of Aboriginal children in remote parts of the NT. Without the word *murder* such a statement was apparently not libellous, probably since it was factual.

The next time I met John was in Canberra in the late eighties. He was then Director of the ACT Council of Social Service (ACTCOSS) and putting the finishing touches to his PhD thesis. I was suffering from Ross River Fever, which I had contracted while teaching a course for Aboriginal welfare workers in Darwin, and I was quite ill. John took me for a delightful day's fishing on a lake near Canberra and we had a nice chin-wag. I was amazed to learn that John had had no difficulties with his employers or the law since we had last met, but I was pleased to note that he had maintained the same fiery condemnation of oppression. Perhaps at ACTCOSS John had at last found an employer who shared his values, or perhaps writing his PhD thesis left no time to get into trouble.

John was awarded a PhD in 1989 and stayed in Canberra as the Director of ACTCOSS until 1993 when he was appointed Senior Lecturer in Social Policy and Community Work at the Queensland University of Technology. We met again briefly in the nineties when I was attending a conference in Brisbane and we had a pleasant afternoon and evening together. The one or two interactions I witnessed between John and his students were ample evidence that he was passing on his radical social work ideas to the next generation of receptive students.

John retired in 2007 and remains active in supporting civil liberties and a Guaranteed Minimum Income. He continues to campaign for a better treatment of asylum seekers, civil rights for Aborigines and a better deal for the poor among many other causes.

John's thinking had a big influence on my early conceptualisation of such issues as social fairness, civil liberties, distribution of wealth, justice and the abuse of power. His ideas took root and flourished in fertile ground, but I never had John's courage to act fearlessly on my convictions. I am very glad to have followed along the trail that he has blazed through Australian society and Australian history.

Bibliography

Tomlinson, John. (1967). *Reflections of a fool*. Darwin: Wobbly Press.

Tomlinson, John. (1974). *Confessions of an opiate eater*. Darwin: Wobbly Press.

Tomlinson, John. (1977). *Is band-aid social work enough?* Darwin: Wobbly Press.

Tomlinson, John. (1982). *Social work community work*. Darwin: Wobbly Press.

Tomlinson, John. (1982). *Betrayed by bureaucracy*. Darwin: Wobbly Press.

Tomlinson, John. (1983), *The death of Phillip Robertson*. Darwin: Wobbly Press.

Tomlinson, John. (1999). *People's poems and songs of struggle*. Darwin: Wobbly Press.

Tomlinson, John. (2002). Income Support for Unemployed People: Human Rights versus Utilitarian Rights. *Journal of Economic and Social Policy*. 6(2). Retrieved from http://epubs.scu.edu.au/jesp/vol6/iss2/3

Tomlinson, John. (2015). Challenging state aggression against Indigenous Australians. In N. Yu and D. Mandell (Eds.), *Subversive social action: extralegal action for social justice*. Waterloo, ON: Wilfrid Laurier University Press.

Links

Cyclone Tracy
https://en.wikipedia.org/wiki/Cyclone_Tracy
http://www.naa.gov.au/collection/fact-sheets/fs176.aspx
http://www.australiangeographic.com.au/blogs/on-this-day/2014/12/on-this-day-in-history-cyclone-tracy

Essington House
https://www.facebook.com/TheNorthernTerritory/posts/609436789152284

Returning Nola
http://www.cbc.ca/radio/thecurrent/the-current-for-may-18-2016-1.3587149/social-workers-have-a-duty-to-skirt-edge-of-the-law-says-author-1.3587329

Tomlinson Publications
http://trove.nla.gov.au/people/535680?c=people

Stobie poles
https://en.wikipedia.org/wiki/Stobie_pole

East Timor
https://en.wikipedia.org/wiki/Indonesian_invasion_of_East_Timor

Frank Hardy
https://en.wikipedia.org/wiki/Frank_Hardy

Basic income
http://www.basicincome.qut.edu.au/about-biga/meet-the-people-behind-biga.jsp
https://books.google.com.au/books?id=bSbHAAAAQBAJ&pg=PA304&lpg=PA304&dq=john+tomlinson+social+work&source=bl&ots=ErlPLdQ_lN&sig=cLnO6q0zBd2P5clEFNT5cxNGqd0&hl=en&sa=X&ved=0ahUKEwjAjoCxkLvPAhXDFpQKHZxIAM44HhDoAQgaMAA#v=onepage&q=john%20tomlinson%20social%20work&f=false
http://epubs.scu.edu.au/cgi/viewcontent.cgi?article=1031&context=jesp

Asylum seekers
http://www.safecom.org.au/pdfs/acadmics-abbott-letter.pdf

Treatment of Aboriginal children
http://search.proquest.com/openview/f18ca4b28a3273bece389f2513f17ff0/1?pq-origsite=gscholar&cbl=1816419

NT intervention
http://treatyrepublic.net/content/northern-territory-intervasion

CHAPTER 19

Ants and the death wish

During the vacation after my second year at university I decided to prepare for my third year by starting to gather data for my independent investigation – a major third year psychology assignment. I did this partly because having failed a subject in second year I would need to pick up an extra subject in third year and it would therefore be a busy year. Having a major assignment completed would take the pressure off.

Also, I had a great idea for an experiment and I couldn't wait to run it and find out the result.

I was intrigued by the experiments that were being run at Duke University in the parapsychology laboratory which indicated that people can predict simple events (such as which card will be dealt next) and could report which card an experimenter is thinking of. These extrasensory perception (ESP) experiments were treated more seriously in the sixties than they are today but in those days they were still dogged by scepticism and outright ridicule in some psychological quarters. The criticisms mainly stemmed from the notion that the subjects (or even the experimenters) were cheating.

But not all psychologists were sceptical. There were rumours in psychological circles that the military was taking ESP and psychic ability very seriously. The Americans and the Russians were reported to be using ESP in their efforts to win the cold war by reading intelligence straight from the minds of the enemy. These rumours circulated alongside other disturbing ideas such as the use of brainwashing as an interrogation technique. Soon after that other rumours circulated suggesting that the first rumours were nonsense and no respectful psychologist would pay any credence to them.

It was only years later that more details became widely known with the publication of material such as Ronson's (2004) book *The Men Who Stare at*

Goats. Ronson claims that starting in the fifties the US military experimented with a wide variety of paranormal techniques including ESP. Some of them, such as attempts to walk through walls or to kill at a distance through concentrated mind power seem merely far-fetched. Other techniques such as the use of loud music as an interrogation technique are more sinister and according to Ronson were the precursor to the torture techniques used at Abu Ghraib.

There is some question as to how factual Ronson's book is. Ronson himself claims that there is more truth in his book than you might think, which implies that some of it is fictitious. And some of it isn't.

Other authors before and since Ronson have made similar claims. In fact typing *paranormal military* into your favorite search engine will yield over 10 million results.

Whatever the truth of Ronson's claims turns out to be, in the early sixties ESP research was somewhat controversial and I thought that producing some definitive evidence would be quite interesting.

My great idea was to reduce the possibility of cheating in an ESP experiment by using animals as subjects rather than people. It is unlikely that animals would try to influence the result of an experiment (except perhaps by trying to escape) and this might lend greater credibility to the results.

It was known that some animals responded to information that could not be picked up through the usual senses and that some could react to impending earthquakes and cyclones and even to the impending sickness or death of a carer. Rhine the reputed father of ESP had written in 1934

The number of reported cases of animal ESP is large enough to suggest that animals can somehow be affected by circumstances they could not be aware of by any sensory sign and which one would suppose they could hardly understand in human terms.

So it was not too fanciful an idea that the amount of ESP animals displayed could be quantified.

I spent some time trying to come up with a simple and convincing experiment that would not take too long. I didn't have the time to train animals to respond to various stimuli so I decided that I would have to be looking for a reaction to a premonition of being harmed in some way.

I didn't want to harm sentient animals and this gave me pause for some time until I realised that I could use insects as my experimental subjects. I didn't mind harming insects; I had killed hundreds of flies, mosquitoes and cockroaches in my time.

There were thousands of ants around my parent's house that summer so I settled on ants. And to give them a really solid danger to react to I decided that the unlucky ants would be killed.

The test would be so see if the ants could predict that being in one bowl of honey would be dangerous and in the other would be safe.

I set up two dishes containing honey next to each other equidistant from the ant nest. After half an hour I tossed a coin to determine which bowl of ants would live and which die. Then I killed the ants in the designated bowl and set the others free.

The results were astounding. Over many trials the number of ants entering the safe and dangerous bowls differed by a huge amount. The results were statistically significant well beyond the strictest test of probability.

Unfortunately the results were in the opposite direction to my prediction. If the ants had ESP they also had a death wish of monumental proportions.

This presented me with a big problem: how could these results be written up?

If the results had been the other way round I could have written up an experiment supporting Rhine's anecdotal evidence that animals were *affected by circumstances they could not be aware of by any sensory sign:* a startling conclusion supported by evidence and therefore acceptable even if unconventional.

If there had been no difference between the numbers of ants in the two bowls I could have written up the results suggesting that ants didn't seem to have ESP; a perfectly acceptable result for a conservative psychology department.

But the result of this experiment implied that the ants knew they were going to die and welcomed it. I found this impossible to explain sensibly and the few people I discussed it with reacted as though I had confirmed their worst fears of my character and intellect. In the end I couldn't find a way of writing up that would not have the likely result of my failing this part of the course and ruining my reputation so I reluctantly gave it up.

This was possibly my first lesson in the importance of politics, prejudice and beliefs to the progress of science. Beliefs, prejudices and politics may only have a small effect on the results of experiments but they have a profound influence on what gets reported.

To this day I observe ants and notice that they seem to be able to predict wet weather and they change the colour of the tiny stones on their nest according to how much sunlight they expect each day in order to regulate the temperature of the nest.

And I still wonder: what is it with ants and the death wish?

Bibliography

Rhine, J. B. (1934). *Extra-Sensory Perception*. Boston, MA: Bruce Humphries.

Ronson, Jon. (2004). *The Men Who Stare at Goats*. London: Picador, Pan Macmillan.

CHAPTER 20

Getting hooked on science

Third year psychology at Queensland University in the sixties had two strands in much the same way as second year. The theoretical strand had a subject that got my full attention: visual perception.

Having only one fully working eye (and that one very long sighted) I was intrigued by the way that eyes were supposed to work compared with the way that mine actually worked. I still love the optical illusions and the way the mind can play tricks with visual input. I was especially intrigued by the ones that did not work with someone who has only one functioning eye.

This part of the course was taught by Laurie Enticknap whose passion for the intrigues of visual perception made his lectures and tutorials a constant adventure for me.

Laurie also gave me the opportunity to recover from my *ants and the death wish* debacle by providing me with a very practical experimental project. I can't remember exactly how this came about – he may have called for volunteers or he may have approached me directly. Either way the result was the same – I became an unpaid lab assistant with a budget and more or less free scope to carry out the experiment as I saw fit.

The project was to determine whether people judged the strength of cordial flavour by taste or sight. At first flush it seems obvious that people would judge the strength of a cordial by its taste, but it turned out that the colour density of the cordial was far more influential. My experiment showed that a weakly flavoured cordial that is highly coloured will be judged as tasting strongly flavoured by almost everybody.

Laurie might have intended to write a paper on this at some stage using the data I collected, or it may simply have been that he had a bet with the local cordial manufacturer. Either way, I'm sure that you have noticed that soft drinks and cordials are massively over coloured these days. I feel at least partly responsible. This guilt is compensated for to a certain extent by the acquisition of three dozen sherry glasses and several cordial flavours and colours, part of the experimental equipment, which lasted me for more than a decade of social gatherings.

It may have been the plan that I should write up this experiment for my third year project, but I decided against that. Studying the influence of one sense over another had opened up a whole new area of speculation for me.

How extraordinary that a strong colour can actually make a cordial *taste* stronger. I wondered whether the senses interacted in this way in other situations. Did vision always win? If vision was being fooled but another sense was accurate, did vision still always win? To make a start I decided to find out if visual illusions could be replicated in other senses and whether the illusion in one sense would affect how something is interpreted by another sense. This line of approach seemed to open up limitless possibilities.

When I started to think about it in more detail it became obvious that I had set myself a difficult task when I decided to replicate visual illusions in other sensory modalities. For example if you place arrowheads on the ends of a line it will appear to be a different length. A nice example of this is at http://www.michaelbach.de/ot/sze-muelue/index.html

This is a compelling visual illusion. Even when you know the lines are the same length they still look different lengths. My problem was – how could I turn this into a taste illusion or a touch illusion or an auditory illusion.

From my current vantage point I can see how it might be done for an auditory illusion. With modern acoustic equipment it would be possible to add pieces to a sound bite to make it seem shorter or longer or apparently change pitch. Such effects can be created these days, but back then I didn't know about them, and probably the technology available was not capable of producing them.

After working on the problem for another eight years or so I became sophisticated enough to solve a small conundrum in the early seventies. I was approached by an ornithologist with a recording of a bird call that didn't make sense. The recording, of a whip bird I think, was of a long call with a whip like crack at the end. What didn't make sense is that the oscilloscope representation of the recording showed another sound was consistently occurring between the long call and the whip crack – but no matter how we tried none of us could hear it. The sound was obviously there on the oscilloscope and its amplitude indicated that it should be audible, but we couldn't hear it.

I worked out that this was an example of backward masking. When a loud sound occurs at exactly the right time following a short, soft sound, the short sound is masked. I had never heard of this happening outside of human experience so it was quite a discovery that the whipbird apparently has a secret sound in its song. This discovery of backward masking in whipbirds has since been extended to other animals such as parakeets (Dooling and Searcy, 1980) and even goldfish (Popper and Clarke, 1976). Backward masking it turns out has important implications for how our nervous system works – and may indicate that some information travels faster along the nerve fibres. At least that's one possible explanation for backward masking – the second stronger stimulus travels faster, overtakes the first one and wipes it out. I think the jury is still out on that one – it may be a lot more complicated.

Back in the sixties as a third year student I was not so well informed and it took me some time to come up with an optical illusion that could be replicated in touch and hearing. I settled on the autokinetic effect as my illusion of choice. Just working out why this illusion occurs kept me interested for another six years (four of them fulltime) till I finally nailed it.

The autokinetic illusion is easy to set up. All you need is a completely dark room and a tiny pinpoint of light. If you watch the light for a few minutes it will appear to move around. No one knew why, but I was not interested in that at that stage. I wanted to find out if a continuous noise would also appear to move around. It did.

This was much more satisfying than studying the death wish of prescient ants. Sometime during that year I became hooked on running experiments – an obsession that has lasted for the rest of my life.

Given the chance I'll measure and test anything you care to name.

Bibliography

Dooling, R.J. & Searcy, M.H. Forward and backward auditory masking in the parakeet (Melopsittacus undulatus). *Hearing Research*, 3, 279-84.

Popper, A.N. (1976). The auditory system of the goldfish (*Carassius auratus*): effects of intense acoustic stimulation. *Comparative Biochemistry and Physiology,* 53A, 11-18.

Link

Muller-Lyer arrowhead illusion
http://www.michaelbach.de/ot/sze-muelue/index.html

CHAPTER 21

Laurie Enticknap and speed reading

An invaluable help in reading for my PhD was a speed-reading course I did with Laurie Enticknap. It has also been immensely useful to me over the last fifty years of professional life.

Laurie was one of those people that you find in most psychology departments who seem to be involved in a low-key way with just about everything that is happening in the department. He didn't push himself forward, but his opinion was often sought and he often assisted with other people's projects as well as conducting many of his own. In his career he worked and published in areas as diverse as perception, electronics, statistics, aging, child welfare and speech.

In the mid sixties there were a number of speed-reading courses being heavily advertised – particularly to university students. Laurie Enticknap ran a series of experiments to determine if any of those courses did improve reading speed and accuracy as advertised and if so which was the most effective.

The courses used a number of techniques to teach people how to read faster. Some instructed the reader to look only at the beginning of each line, some to look only at the middle. Some suggested reading only the first few words of each paragraph. Some even had a mechanical device, which allowed only one line of text to be in view, and ran down the page at a fixed speed. Each course favoured a particular method and had its own hype to explain how it worked and why it was superior.

Laurie asked separate groups of students to engage in each of the different speed reading courses and assessed the results with two measures. The time taken to read a standard number of words was the speed measure in words per minute (wpm). The comprehension measure was the percentage of correct answers to a series of questions about the content of each test paragraph.

The courses took several weeks and progress was measured at standard intervals.

I was fortunate to be in the control group. A control group is used in experiments to see what effect going through the motions has. It usually comprises an activity that seems like the experimental condition but lacks the vital ingredient that is supposed to produce the effect.

In Laurie's experiment the control group was given the same exercises as the experimental groups, but with none of the techniques that were supposed to teach you how to read faster. Instead, subjects were issued with a rather bland Zen like instruction: *read faster*.

Laurie found no difference between the groups with regards to improvement in either speed of reading or comprehension. This may lead you to believe that none of those speed-reading courses worked and in one sense this is true. Differences in technique did not make any difference. On the other hand the reading speed and comprehension of all the subjects improved. Even those in the control group!

In my case my speed improved from around 200wpm (which is average) to well over 1000wpm (which is well above average). At the same time my comprehension improved to above 80%.

So the conclusion I would draw from these results is that improvement in speed and comprehension are not dependent on technique, but are probably simply a result of the intention to read faster.

So it's probably a waste of money to buy a speed-reading course. If you want to read faster, just…read faster.

Of course it is very handy to have a set of test passages and comprehension questions so you can get some feedback as to how you are progressing. You can find those for free on the net and I have listed some of them in the bibliography section for this chapter. Be warned though that some of these are on websites that will eventually try to sell you a speed-reading course.

For interest's sake as I was preparing this chapter I took the speed reading test at *Reading test online* at http://www.readingsoft.com/ and was surprised to find after all these years that my speed is still a respectable 725wpm and my comprehension is at 82%. Although I have used speed-reading a lot in the last fifty years I haven't made any attempt to practice reading faster and yet my scores are still well above my starting point. This is obviously a skill that holds up well with age.

Over the years I have used speed reading to absorb the content of journal articles, books, technical and clinical reports, hospital charts, DIY instructions, and the dust jackets of novels. It saves a lot of time and I find I can still absorb the information at speed.

There is a very large downside to speed-reading when it comes to reading for pleasure. I soon found that reading poetry and novels was eerily bland. Speed-reading enabled me to acquire all the information in a novel, but none of the colour. I could read a novel in half a day and be quite clear about the plot and characterisation, but I got none of the emotional connection with the characters and story that I enjoy so much when reading novels.

I eventually worked out that the emotional connection takes time and I would have to slow down to get it. It took me quite some time to learn to control the speed of my read and eventually developed two *gears,* one for work and one for pleasure.

So I do hope that you don't speed read this memoir – you won't enjoy reading it half as much.

I am really grateful to Laurie Enticknap for giving me the opportunity to learn to speed-read. I also remember him warmly for his skill in teaching perception, which set me on the path to the autokinetic illusion and my PhD.

Bibliography

Enticknap, L E. (1960). The Decade-Counter Tube in the Psychological Laboratory. *American Journal of Psychology,* 73(1), 138. Retrieved from http://search.proquest.com/openview/b68aaa739b98a0623fdf7041427cd933/1?pq-origsite=gscholar&cbl=1821530

Harwood, E. & Enticknap, L. E. (1984). Longitudinal Study Of Intelligence: The Sixteenth Year In "Operation Retirement". *Australian Journal on Ageing,* 3(3), 20–22.

Hills, I. M., An interesting take on speed reading, 2016, *Education Watch International.* At http://edwatch.blogspot.com.au/

Naylor, G.F.K. & Enticknap, L.E. (1981). *Statistics simplified: An introduction for social scientists and others.* London: Harcourt Brace Jovanovich.

Links

Speed reading
http://www.readingsoft.com/
http://projects.wsj.com/speedread/
http://www.staples.com/sbd/cre/marketing/technology-research-centers/ereaders/speed-reader/
http://mindbluff.com/askread.htm
https://en.wikipedia.org/wiki/Speed_reading

CHAPTER 22

Statistical Encounters

In the early sixties measurement theory and statistics was taught to third year psychology students by Dr John Keats and Professor Donald McElwain who fired my interest in mathematics, statistics, measurement and the scientific method. Both these teachers were well-respected experts in their field; in fact they had recently published a modification of a new statistical technique called *unfolding* (McElwain & Keats, 1961) which we analysed and discussed in and out of class.

I found their approach appealing not only because it was simple to apply, but also because of the rather cute area they applied it to – the radio listening preferences of Brisbane schoolchildren. The remarkable results they obtained occasioned the most discussion (on a metaphysical rather than statistical plane). Their results indicated that the placement of radio stations in the mathematical space of children's radio preferences corresponded closely to the placement of radio stations on the wireless dial – and gave me an early bemused introduction to Jung's world of meaningful coincidence.

Unfolding technique allows for stimuli and subjects to be distributed in the same mathematical space. The technique represented a step forward in statistical analysis in that previously most correlational factor analysis techniques allowed only stimuli to be distributed. Factor analysis gives a good idea of which variables *hang together* but much less information as to how subjects are distributed over those variables. In addition, *unfolding* is a non-parametric technique – thus avoiding the pitfalls of applying parametric factor analysis to questionably parametric data.

Finally – the coup de grace – unfolding technique is easy to compute compared with the cumbersome factor analysis.

Bear in mind that in those days, before the wide availability of computers and SPSS, factor analysis involved interminable multiplying and squaring of long lists of numbers to obtain correlation coefficients followed by further mathematical manipulation of the coefficients to obtain factors. Even a reasonably limited factor analysis could take weeks hunched over a calculator, with reams of paper, eye strain, brain strain, hundreds of cups of coffee and complaints of neglect from loved ones.

And if you are thinking, "surely this could all be done on a computer", well yes it could but not much easier. The computer centre at University of Queensland at that time was several stories high and attended by operators in white lab coats who behaved like priests at the shrine of data and prevented anyone else from approaching the god-computer; an impressive grandiloquence for a computer with a tiny fraction of the power of the desktop computer on which I am typing this account. This state-of-the-art computer ran on valves just like the 1960s radios and was very bulky (just like the 1960s radios). Desktops, laptops, ipads, and ipods were not even dreamed of – except perhaps by Dick Tracy fans who hoped that one day there would be a phone that you could carry round with you.

To complete a factor analysis (or indeed any analysis) using an early sixties computer required punching the data onto computer cards. The punching was literal. Each letter, number, comma or backslash in each line of data became a slot shaped hole punched in a specific position on a data card, one card per line, through the mechanical magic of a multiple card punch. Transferring the data from your lab records to the cards could take several days.

The cards were then taken to the computer centre – being very careful not to drop the box containing hundreds of cards. If you did it could take several hours, or even days, to put them back in the correct order. After my first dropped box I decided to number the cards in felt pen as they were produced. This adds to the punching time, but saves a lot of time in event of a drop. If the cards are not numbered in this way, re-sorting them into order meant holding each card up to the light and reading the holes punched in it to figure out what the line might say, then referring back to the written data list to work out where that card should go; tedious, boring work that seemed to take for ever.

When leaving the cards with the priests in white lab coats at the computer centre one could get an estimate of when they were likely to run your job: usually in about a week. Returning a week later you could pick up a thick wad of computer paper - paper designed to be as inconvenient to work with as is possible - about a yard wide with holes down the side with the pages stacked concertina style along the perforated edges. Taking this stack of hundreds of connected pages to a large table – usually in a laboratory – you could pore over it for a couple of hours trying to work out where the results were hidden and eventually discover that the tiny words printed on the final page *error in line 16* meant that there was something wrong with the input cards and the job had not run.

Examining the cards carefully, eventually you would discover that you had left out a comma or a backslash on one of the cards. After preparing and inserting a replacement card it's off to the computer centre for another run. Often it would take three or four goes to get a successful run. As the weeks passed you realised that you could have completed the analysis by hand by now. And eventually you did. It was nice to get the computer's confirmation of your analysis a few weeks later, just to be sure that you hadn't made any mistakes.

Given the complications and time involved in computing a factor analysis in the early sixties it is not surprising that unfolding technique became quite popular, and not just for sixties third year psychology students. Subsequently this technique and its later derivatives were used in analysing data from economics (e.g. Wedel and Steenkamp, 1989) and particle physics (e.g. Blobel, 1984) as well as the social sciences (e.g. Habing, et al, 2005).

Later in the seventies at James Cook University my colleague Mike Smithson wrote a new computer program for a technique called *smallest space analysis* developed by Lingoes (1966), which also places subjects and stimuli in the same mathematical space. As a test of Mikes new program we had some fun analysing data from the 16PF handbook showing the profiles associated with a number of mental health disorders. This analysis yielded dimensions bearing a remarkable resemblance to the factors of Osgood's semantic differential (warm-cold, strong-weak etc). We wrote a paper entitled *Catell Meets Osgood: a multidimensional analysis of personality profiles underlying mental disorders*, but sadly couldn't find a publisher for it. It now languishes in a large section of my filing cabinet labeled *unpublished*.

Mike continues to publish prolifically in a number of fields including statistics and social science, and his site can be accessed at http://psychology.anu.edu.au/about-us/people/mike-smithson#acton-tabs-link--tabs-0-middle-1

Details of his latest book *Generalized Linear Models for Categorical and Continuous Limited Dependent Variables* written with Ed Merkle can be found at http://statistics.crcpress.com/new-notable/generalized-linear-models/

I have to say that I've always enjoyed playing with numbers ever since I read *Mathematics for the Million* when I was around 12 years old and this fascination has fitted nicely with my interest in psychology – the two go hand in glove. I've been very lucky in this regard I think. I have met psychologists who struggle with the statistical side of our discipline and feel that they are at a disadvantage. So much of what we have discovered in psychology depends on statistical analysis and understanding advances in our science as they occur depends on a good grasp of the mathematics underlying the analysis of data. To actually enjoying the process of unpicking the analysis is a huge advantage.

My enjoyment of and my early training in statistics have allowed me to apply the psychological version of the scientific method to much of my work as a psychologist. Whatever I have been involved in I have usually found a way of measuring progress towards a goal and this makes it easy to judge how effective I have been. I have found this a very good learning tool allowing me to find out at first hand what works for me and what is failing to produce the desired result.

Of all my teachers McElwain and Keats contributed most to my use and enjoyment of this process.

Bibliography

Bennett, J. F. (1956). Determination of the number of independent parameters of a score matrix from the examination of rank orders. *Psychometrika*, 21, 383–393.

Blobel, V. (1984). Unfolding methods in high energy physics experiments, Report DESY 84-118,

Habing, B. Finch, H. & Roberts, J. (2005). *A Q3 Statistic for Unfolding Item Response Theory Models: Assessment of Unidimensionality With Two Factors and Simple Structure. Applied Psychological Measurement*, 29(6), 457-471.

Hogben, L. (1936). *Mathematics for the Million*. London: Allen & Unwin.

Lingoes, J. C. (1996). An IBM 7090 Program for Guttman-Lingoes Smallest Space Analysis-III. *Behavioral Science*, 11, 75-76.

McElwain, D.W. & Keats, J.A. (1961). Multidimensional unfolding: some geometrical solutions. *Psychometrika*, 26(3), 325-332.

Smithson, M. & Merkle, E.C. (2013). *Generalized Linear Models for Categorical and Continuous Limited Dependent Variables*. Boca Raton, Florida: Chapman and Hall.

Wedel, M. & Steenkamp, J.B.E.M. (1989), Fuzzy clusterwise regression approach to benefit segmentation. *International Journal of Research in Marketing,* 6, 241-258.

Links

Hogben's Mathematics for the Million, free download
http://www.muebooks.com/mathematics-for-the-million-with-answers-PDF-4793931/

Mike Smithson
http://psychology.anu.edu.au/about-us/people/mike-smithson#acton-tabs-link--tabs-0-middle-1

CHAPTER 23

Professorial Influence

As a student I was aware of Professor McElwain as a distant, avuncular, authoritative figure in the Psychology Department at Queensland University. Although he held regular staff meetings, and we students were conscious that important decisions that affected our academic lives were made at these meetings, it seemed clear that the Professor was in charge and had the final say.

At some stage I learned to refer to him as Mac rather than the more formal Professor, so I will refer to him in this way here. This way of referring to him reflects more accurately the fondness and respect I have for him. Mac had a profound influence on my development as a psychologist and as a person especially when I became a postgraduate student and was supervised by him.

Mac was quietly spoken, calm, comfortable and yet imposing man. He dressed casually and smoked a pipe – in appearance almost a caricature of the avuncular psychologist - a modern day shaman.

I have been told that Mac's management style was somewhat *laissez faire* and that he tended to agree with whatever proposal was being suggested to him at the time, giving the impression that he often changed his mind. I have also been told that he was authoritarian and could not be persuaded from his chosen course. Perhaps people saw in him what they wanted or needed to see, perhaps he was able to operate in both these styles.

In the mid sixties when student unrest was beginning to affect the relationship between staff and students Mac presided over a series of departmental meetings, which unusually for the time included both staff and students. All staff and students were invited to attend. Since the Department then comprised well over a thousand students and scores of staff, the meetings were of necessity huge and interminable.

Mac and the staff sat at a table in a small, claustrophobic lecture theatre. Students sat in the gallery. In retrospect the seating arrangement seems to reflect the problems being addressed. On the one hand *authority* was reaching out to bridge the gap between staff and students. On the other hand the structure of authority was being maintained and demonstrated. Most of the talking was done by the students and most of the listening was done by the staff in a production that could easily have been the prototype for a modern complaints process.

I was not privy to the decisions that resulted from that series of meetings but I'm reasonably sure that many of the ideas that governed the further development of the Department had their genesis in those ventilation sessions. In any event it is clear that in the latter half of the sixties the Queensland University Psychology Department had a relatively untroubled time while in other areas students became more and more rebellious. Those meetings probably helped a lot.

On a more personal level a postgraduate student once told me that Mac's initial comment on a completed thesis chapter was *it's too wordy*. After the student diligently tightened the writing until it was much shorter Mac's comment was *too terse*. The student then rewrote chapter to medium length and presented the first two versions at the next session with the comment *are you in a long or short mood today?* and then trumped the reply with the third middle-sized version. Mac took it in good part.

Considering his background and experience Mac was the obvious choice to establish a Psychology Department at Queensland University in 1955. He had already set up a successful department of psychology at Melbourne University, he had a wide experience of psychology and had previously been both an academic and in leadership roles in the army during World War ll.

Mac was a man with a wide range of interests and by 1955 at only 40 years of age he already had worked in areas as diverse as cognitive testing, vocational selection, educational psychology, cross cultural psychology, veterans mental health and management psychology and had published in most of these areas. By the end of his career these interests had expanded to include dozens of publications in areas as diverse as statistics, child welfare, the psychology of art, cross cultural selection, anthropology, social psychology, cross cultural sick role behaviour among many others. His influence in encouraging a broad range of interests was apparent not only in the very wide range of research that was conducted in the department, (ranging from visual perception to sexual behaviour) but also in the gradually expanding course offerings that eventually led to the establishment of the School of Social Sciences.

I have to say that this approach suited me down to the ground and like Mac's my interests have expanded over the years. I have an investigative mind and a tendency to get bored once I have mastered a skill and this has led me to try lots of different ways of being a psychologist. I have worked as an academic, researcher and teacher; and practised in many areas of psychology including clinical, forensic, neurological, vocational, drug and alcohol treatment, organisational, cross-cultural, educational, counselling and community work. Mac's influence is easy to detect in my career path and I dare say in the careers of other students of my cohort.

I thought this approach to a career path was universally accepted as laudable until sometime in the eighties when my boss referred to me disparagingly as a *renaissance man* after hearing that I was attempting to learn basic Arrernte and Pitjantjatjara as preparation for working with Aborigines in central Australia. More recently my employees and students were rather bemused to find me doing my own plumbing repairs and changing my own light bulbs.

CHAPTER 24

More about Mac

It is thanks to Mac's influence that I was surprised to realise that most people think that intense specialisation is a higher calling than wide general skill. Professed lack of skill in areas outside ones speciality is generally considered a mark of distinction rather than a lack of a broad education.

Mac's easy ability to take an interest in a wide range of fields encouraged me to do the same and accept it as customary. As a result I have been able to change my focus many times and psychology has held my fascinated interest for nearly 50 years.

It was also clear that Mac thought that it was a good thing for psychologists to have a range of extra-curricular interests. It was common knowledge that Mac was a keen potter and many of his students followed his lead in this. In fact at least one of the students in my University cohort left psychology soon after graduation to become a fulltime potter.

Mac was also a keen chess player and many within the Department brushed up their skills to join in. Once, when he was hospitalised, Mac invited students to visit specifically to play chess with him, which many of us did. Even when ill he was very difficult to beat. Others in the department also played social games of five hundred in which I occasionally joined.

I'm sure Mac's example and encouragement to maintain a wide range of extra-curricular interests provided me with protection from burnout later in my career, as the internal stresses of clinical work built up over time. In the seventies Mike Smithson, one of my colleagues at James Cook University, commented that I used song writing to *scrape my shit off the walls* and get it into a neat pile where I could deal with it properly. He was right.

I continue to play chess and later backgammon for a similar purpose – I find that the level of concentration required clears my mind of extraneous disturbing thoughts.

My main diversion was guitar playing, song writing and performing – activities that I pursued until recently arthritis and *guitarist's neck* made it too difficult to play for more than a few minutes at a time. Now I am learning to play other musical instruments that rely on body parts that still function effectively enough, but I miss the ready skill that I had with the guitar.

It was clear that Mac had the long-term interests of the Department as a main focus and the Department went from strength to strength under his leadership growing in size and stature over the years. He was also greatly concerned with the welfare of his students and staff and put effort into providing a social setting for the Department. There were Departmental outings – often centred on research projects or conferences, and senior students were provided with a home room even though accommodation was at a premium. Higher degree students were routinely offered lab space, a workroom and a part-time teaching position to supplement the rather meagre Commonwealth Scholarship living allowance.

One could imagine that Mac's interviewing style was influenced by his army training. He had a couple of very effective interviewing tricks that many of us copied and found useful in our later work as psychologists. The first of these was extended silence. At a crucial moment he would establish eye contact, adopt an air of expectancy and simply sit silent until one felt forced to say something, anything at all, to ease the tension of a long, long, long, awkward moment.

McElwain's second interviewing trick – if the first one didn't work or if the issue was crucial – was to leave the room. He would get up, say something non-committal like "excuse me a moment" and leave the room closing, the door behind him. After five minutes of waiting and wondering, his return to the room was like a reprieve and going over the same ground from a different perspective seemed more or less inevitable if not positively welcome.

I was on the receiving end of both those techniques as a PhD student when Professor McElwain was one of my supervisors. In fact the room-leaving technique was part of the process for my upgrading to the PhD program from the Masters program.

A meeting with the head of department, supervisor and student was *de rigueur* when embarking on a higher degree, to obtain advice on and approval of the proposed research program. Having been awarded a second class honours I was under the impression that I would not be accepted into the PhD program and went along to that meeting with a proposal for a Masters degree. After perusing my proposal and other documents, and asking a few searching questions the Professor made some positive comments about the PhD program, mentioned that there were some places available and suggested that my Commonwealth

Scholarship would cover such a program. Then he stood up and left the room. After a few seconds of stunned silence my supervisor (new to the Department and this tactic) looked at me and said *it looks like you'd better apply for the PhD program*. And so I did.

Bibliography

Kearney, George E. (2000). Obituaries: Donald William McElwain AO, ED, FBPsS, HonFAPS, 1915-2000. *Australian Aboriginal Studies.*

Links

Professor McElwain
http://www.questia.com/library/journal/1G1-72609295/obituaries-donald-william-mcelwain-ao-ed-fbpss
http://www.thefreelibrary.com/OBITUARIES%3A+Donald+William+McElwain+AO,+ED,+FBPsS,+HonFAPS+1915-2000.-a072609295

CHAPTER 25

Measurement Theory

The theoretical strand of third year psychology at Queensland University in the mid-sixties had a large component of measurement theory, which I found fascinating. The course was taught by McElwain and Keats from whom I absorbed an enthusiasm for the subject as well as knowledge about how measurement develops.

As it gradually dawned on me that measurement is simply the process of defining how numbers are assigned to phenomena, I sensed the cogs of the universe shifting. If measurement is simply the process of defining how numbers are assigned to phenomena then any numbers can be assigned to anything and measures are as meaningful or meaningless as the rules of the definition.

When Henry the First of England defined a yard as the distance from his nose to his thumb it was just as valid as the French National Assembly defining a metre as *the length of a pendulum with a half-period of one second* (French National assembly, 1790). The fact that both these definitions have changed several times makes them nonetheless scientific. The measures work as long as you follow the definition and apply the rules correctly.

I realised later that the changes in definition usually follow the discovery of mistakes in the original definition, which paradoxically are discovered only through the application of the original measure. For example when it was discovered that variations in gravity affected the swing of a pendulum the pendulum definition for the metre was superseded by *one twenty-millionth of the length of the Earth's meridian*. This definition was also abandoned when it was discovered that there had been a miscalculation of the flattening of the Earth's surface and the meridian standard was one fifth of a millimetre short. After a couple more tries the current definition is based on a fraction of the speed of light and is thought to be more accurate – at least until someone finds another mistake and comes up with a better definition of a metre.

This definition of a metre also fixes the speed of light but this circularity doesn't seem to bother anyone because over time the measurement rules begin to define the thing being measured.

This counter intuitive logical circularity has led some scientists into the absurdity of claiming that there is no such thing as cold – only the absence of heat. This conclusion is the result of the rules by which we measure temperature, which involved in the first instance measuring the length of a column of mercury in an enclosed tube. The mercury expands and contracts because of the energy imparted by heat. Only heat or absence of heat can influence the length of the mercury – so over time temperature became defined by its measure as equivalent to the presence of a certain amount of heat. According to this conceptualisation of temperature the concept of cold is not necessary and so is by definition held to be non-existent.

As a result my science teacher at high school was able to insist, *There is no such thing as cold – only the absence of heat.* Anyone who has walked barefoot in the snow can testify to the ridiculousness of that idea. Conceptually it is somewhat akin to maintaining that there is no such thing as a hole – only the absence of dirt.

Perhaps as the measurement of temperature continues to improve, and at some stage collides with the notion that sensations can be measured, we will have the concept of cold reintroduced so that we can validate how uncomfortable it feels.

In light of this experiential absurdity resulting from the measurement of temperature it beggars belief that some physical scientists still maintain that psychological measures are unscientific. If the principles of measurement theory are applied to psychological phenomena by carefully defining how numbers are applied to the phenomena, then of course they can be scientifically measured.

The same arguments apply to weight, energy, time and all the other measures we rely on for accurate appraisal of our world. If this makes the laws of physics seem a little more rubbery than I had previously thought, by comparison it makes psychological measurement seem considerably less rubbery.

If something as basic as length can be measured by all agreeing that the size of the earth or the length of an arm is our common unit then we can measure psychological variables such as happiness by agreeing how to assign the numbers. For example to get us started we could all agree that happiness can be measured by asking people how happy they are. If we ask them to rate their happiness out of ten we could agree that the number they assign is the measure.

As long as we all apply the rule the same way it will be a valid measure and, weirdly, over time the numbers will become the definition of happiness.

Of course I hadn't conceptualised it quite as clearly as a third year student. Later for my PhD after much further thought I extended this simple measurement principle and asked people to estimate the illusory movement of a pinpoint of light – i.e. to apply a number to the size of a movement that did not actually occur but only appeared to occur.

It worked well enough for me to be able eventually to explain why a stationary pinpoint of light viewed in darkness appears to move. And it worked well enough to get me a PhD.

Much later while teaching at James Cook University I was approached by an environmental scientist looking for a more efficient way of measuring the health of the Great Barrier Reef. The method then used was to mark off a small area and meticulously measure the areas of live and dead coral within that area. This scientist wanted to measure square miles of reef and did not have the funds or the time to carry out that sort of meticulous measurement. I suggested to him that he could tow his observers face down over an area of reef and ask them to give it a score out of ten. He could then validate this new measure against the previous more meticulous one by comparing the two measures over the same area of reef.

This practical application of measurement theory worked really well for many years but has recently been replaced by the modern method of measuring coral with remote sensing during a plane flyover.

Links

Gas Laws
http://en.wikipedia.org/wiki/Ideal_gas_law

CHAPTER 26

Measurement and clinical practice

In clinical practice I was wedded to the idea of measuring progress towards clinical goals long before it became common practice. I eventually became disenchanted with the global measures of anxiety, depression, social isolation and the like and looked for a way of measuring progress towards the client's stated goals. My previous experience with using basic measurement theory to make difficult measurements came in very handy.

I took an idea from *Problem Oriented Record Keeping* and started recording symptoms as problems to be solved rather than only as signs of pathology. At first I simply asked clients what problems they would like to see solved by the time we concluded a course of therapy. I then combined this with a technique called SUDS (Subjective Units of Distress Scale) and asked the client to rate each problem out of ten, with 0 being not a problem and 10 being the worst that a problem could be.

This process coincidentally had the side benefit of initiating a dialogue to clarify what the problems were and which ones were more important to the client.

I found this very useful in directing my attention to areas of greatest need and in addition as we rated each problem each session it became clear which parts of the treatment were working well and what needed fine-tuning.

Very soon it occurred to me that ratings would be a useful way to set an end point to therapy and that this should be done at the outset. It was clear that the ideal rating for some problems would not be zero. For example, having no anxiety at all about anything would not be a healthy thing – in fact it could prove positively dangerous. It seemed to me that simply asking the client to set an end point might not be entirely satisfactory either since it is possible that a client's unrealistic expectations about their problems might be part of the difficulty. So in the first couple of sessions I negotiated with clients what the ratings should be by the end of the course of treatment. Let's call this the goal rating (G)

I was then able to measure the effectiveness of a course of treatment for each problem presented, to switch focus according to therapeutic need, and to cease therapy at an appropriate point.

Several things became apparent as I applied this recording technique to large numbers of clients. One issue that arose was that as some problems resolved other problems became important to the client. These were handled by simply adding them to the list.

Another issue was that during treatment some client's ratings fell to very close to the goal rating but levelled off just short of the target. In these cases rather than continue unproductively for little or no gain (and perhaps be accused of over servicing) I negotiated an appropriate termination with the client. If the client was happy to reach say 2.25 rather than 2 we could agree to conclude therapy at that point – always with the proviso that the client could return for more sessions at any time.

I found this approach very useful in guiding the progress of therapy but just as importantly over time I was able to collate these ratings from hundreds of clients and make some discoveries about my overall practice. To do this I developed a *success* score for each client. I averaged their ratings over all the problems rated and used these to determine the amount of progress towards the goal, expressed as a percentage.

I used the initial ratings (I) for a starting point, the rating at the final session (F) as the actual achievement and the goal rating (G) as the target aimed for: I-F represents the progress the client achieved in therapy; I-G represents the amount of progress that was set as a goal and $(I-F)/(I-G) \times 100$ is the per cent progress towards the goal.

For example if a client had an average initial rating of 9 (I=9), set a goal of 2 (G=2) and at the final session had an average rating of 2.2 (F=2.2) then the progress towards the goal would be $(9-2.2)/(9-2) \times 100 = 97.14\%$.

Using these progress percentages I was able to discover for example that I was more successful in treating anxiety than depression, that I was very good at treating children with ADHD and SLD and that overall my success rate was close to 90%.

In the early nineties *evidence based practice* was being proposed as a requirement for good clinical practice and by the turn of the millennium it was a definite expectation. Having this collated outcome data meant that I was able to easily fulfil this requirement and provide the evidence that the techniques I was using were effective.

Of course there will be some mathematical objections to me using these numbers in this way. For example I am not able to demonstrate that the SUDS scales that I use to generate the data have interval scale properties and therefore it might not be legitimate to multiply and divide these numbers. I would note that the same objection applies to the common measures of temperature but engineers are still able to use temperature measures in complex calculations, without things blowing up or falling down.

I'll assume, like the engineers, that since these measures work and give me a lot of useful information it must be OK to use them. Most importantly the rules I use to assign numbers to problem severity are totally transparent and replicable. Anybody can do the same and check my work.

In any case I can blame it all on McElwain and Keats for imparting to me in my third year of study the skill, information and enthusiasm for the idea of measuring what appears to be absurd, insubstantial, chimerical and illusory.

CHAPTER 27

The marvellous mind of John Keats

Of my teachers at Queensland University, John Keats, was the one I had the best rapport with. He had a big impact on my development as a psychologist, an academic and as a person.

As well as being an inspiring teacher of a subject I was interested in - measurement theory - I found John the most approachable of the academic staff. I think this was a view shared by others. One of my colleagues described John's role as second in command of the department as a facilitator. While Mac made the difficult professorial decisions, John was the one who made the personal contact and smoothed the ruffled feathers to ensure that things worked out as they should.

Out of class time John would be available for discussion of the finer points of statistics, measurement theory and mathematics. He was fond of setting logical problems, which had the effect of clarifying and expanding my thinking on any number of topics. This was a teaching technique that I later adopted when I took my turn at encouraging clear thinking in my own students.

John also joined students on many of the Department's student outings. On one occasion on leaving Stradbroke Island at the end of a field trip we had a long wait for the barge back to the mainland. John was amusing (and testing) me with a series of logic puzzles ranging from the prisoner's dilemma to a train-shunting problem involving a circular track and different sized carriages and bridges. When I solved this puzzle far too quickly John decided that he had made a mistake in setting the problem and we were both trying out suggestions to make the puzzle more difficult using a 44 gallon drum to represent the train track.

Neither of us noticed the passing of time, or the fact that the barge had arrived and had loaded vehicles and passengers, until it started raising its ramp and was moving slowly away from the pier. We both ran for the ramp and scrambled aboard to the cheers of the other passengers and the crew.

If you are interested to find out what had us so engrossed that we nearly missed the barge we were standing right next to, the train track puzzle is puzzle number 7 at http://justpuzzles.wordpress.com/2012/02/24/railway-problems/

In this puzzle there is a circular track with a branch line. On each side of a bridge on the circular track there is a carriage (A and B), which cannot fit under the bridge. A single engine (E) that can fit under the bridge is on the connecting branch line. The task is to use the engine to swap the carriages and leave the engine on the branch line.

By all means stop reading now and have a go at this puzzle so that you can get the flavour of a conversation with John Keats on the pier at Stradbroke in the sixties.

These train puzzles were more interesting and relevant in the sixties when steam trains and manual points were still used on suburban lines in Brisbane and shunting could be seen taking place as you passed by the yards at Roma Street. My commute from home included an hour's steam train ride to Roma Street where I changed trains to Toowong, followed by a twenty-minute brisk walk to the University campus, so I was very familiar with trains and shunting. I still retain a strong romantic attachment to trains – especially the old steam driven ones – and my favourite holidays include a long train ride.

Train puzzles along with a raft of other puzzles were a favourite of test constructors such as John who had spent his early career working for ACER and on other test construction projects and did his PhD on cognitive development.

The prisoner's dilemma puzzle is now more usually referred to as Knights and Naves to distinguish it from the better known game theory exercise used to illustrate cooperation and conflict. The puzzle became known as Knights and Naves after its appearance in a wonderful book of puzzles published by Raymond Smullyan in 1978, which I can recommend as a safeguard against boredom. The puzzle was still known by its older name of prisoner's dilemma at the time that John and I were playing with it.

In this puzzle a prisoner is faced with two doors and two guards. One door leads to freedom and the other to death and the prisoner must go through one of the doors. One guard always tells the truth and the other always tells a lie. The prisoner can ask one of the guards one question. The problem is to work out what question will enable the prisoner to work out which door to go through.

In case this puzzle gives you sleepless nights trying to work it out, you will find some clues at http://en.wikipedia.org/wiki/Raymond_Smullyan under the heading *Logic Problems*.

I have retained my penchant for puzzle solving from an early age and this shared interest with John created an easy familiarity that was unusual between lecturers and students in those days. In later years I emulated John both in using logic puzzles to sharpen my students' thinking and in encouraging familiarity with my students.

John had some vulnerabilities and I admired the way he coped with these and made no fuss over them. On one occasion he had an asthma attack during a class. His breathing became quite audible with a whooping asthmatic wheeze. John continued teaching between gasps, while the rest of us were wondering at what point to call an ambulance.

On another occasion John noticed me walking by his laboratory and called me in to examine telephone wires he had rigged in an elaborate three-dimensional array to represent data points. There were dozens of these fine wires coloured in complicated patterns – each wire with a different colour pattern. A brilliant idea for representing a complicated three-dimensional array I thought. Unfortunately John was mildly colour blind, so every now and then he lost track of whether a particular wire was brown, red and yellow or green, blue and yellow and asked a passing student to help him identify the wires. He made no fuss about this problem. His demeanour was that this was just a bloody nuisance that impeded his work, easily solved by asking someone to assist.

I admired John's approach to personal limitations and gradually learned to emulate it. As a person with restricted vision, poor coordination and spelling disability I had previously tried to ignore these limitations. From John I learned to work with them. A few years later when I started to teach at University level I was able to simply admit my problem with spelling and coordination ask my students to correct my sometimes-illegible blackboard scribblings. Years later I attended a seminar in which the presenter explained with a straight face that she was unable to spell whilst standing up. I like that dry humour and I've used that approach myself several times.

John was a man of many talents and had interests in test construction, cross-cultural psychology, mathematics, cognitive development and psychometrics to name but a few. His publications in those areas have often represented conceptual shifts that have resulted in major advances. John's wide range of interests like Mac's (the head of the department) became a model for my own career path which has also ranged over a wide range of psychological and other activities.

It was a sad thing for me when John left the University of Queensland in 1965 to become the foundation professor of Psychology at Newcastle University. Newcastle's gain was definitely Queensland's loss. At the time I was just beginning my fourth year (Honours) studies in psychology and if he had still been at University of Queensland, or I had been able to move to Newcastle, he could well have been my PhD supervisor.

Bibliography

McElwain, D.W. & Keats, J.A. (1961), Multidimensional unfolding: some geometrical solutions. *Psychometrika,* 26 (3), 325-332.

Links

Puzzles
http://justpuzzles.wordpress.com/2012/02/24/railway-problems/
http://en.wikipedia.org/wiki/Raymond_Smullyan

CHAPTER 28

Elsie Harwood and Clinical Psychology

In the early sixties the entire practical strand of third year psychology at the University of Queensland was devoted to clinical psychology. Elsie Harwood conducted most if not all of the training in clinical psychology – assisted by her tutor Lex Irvine. We learned to conduct and analyse a broad range of clinical tests and to write up psychological reports. We learned about the importance of establishing rapport and administering the tests strictly according to the instructions.

Elsie was a person that I much admire, but I'm afraid I did not warm to her as a teacher. In fact I felt somewhat intimidated by her. On first sight you could have taken Elsie for a sixties housewife – with a touch of military discipline. She dressed conventionally in subdued colours and wore sensible shoes. She always had her long hair pulled tightly back in a neat bun. It did not take long to notice the sparkle of intense intelligence that animated her speech and manner signalling that there was a lot more to Elsie than met the eye.

To outward appearances Elsie had no romantic attachments but to some it was inconceivable that a middle-aged University lecturer would be without a love life in the swinging sixties. There was a persistent rumour that she and George Naylor – also a lecturer in the psychology department – were intimately involved. However, this rumour seemed to be based entirely on the observation that Elsie and George drove identical cream coloured Mayflowers.

Elsie was a meticulous teacher. She spent many hours ensuring that we were conducting the tests properly, giving each student individual attention and correcting errors until our performance was perfect. I was dismayed (and a bit surprised) to find that I look intimidating if I peer over my glasses at my test subject, and I was slightly abashed when Elsie pointed it out to me. I spent hours practising how to say numbers at the precise rate of one per second, laying out puzzles in the exact arrangement shown in the manual and learning to say instructions word for word so that Elsie could give me the tick of approval to move on to the next stage.

The next stage was to perform a large number of practice runs (I think it was 10) on friends and family to become very familiar with the WAIS. We all became very skilled at administering this test. Perhaps more important was the underlying message that learning to administer a psychological test requires more that just reading the manual and a looking at the equipment. It requires hours of practice until the instructions and test layout become second nature.

This message stayed with me for the rest of my career as I learned how to administer dozens of tests and to teach the basics of test administration to my students and supervisees. As with Elsie's students, none of my students considered themselves competent in test administration until they had performed a WAIS perfectly under my observation.

Elsie's clinical course included a lot of instruction on what is now referred to as neuropsychology. We learned about the specific functions of the areas of the brain and what cognitive tests tapped into which areas. We also became familiar with EEG brain wave studies and even conducted a number of EEG studies on the second-hand EEG machine that Elsie had acquired for the department.

In the sixties before the advent of brain scans most of the information relating cognitive skills to areas of the brain came from testing people with known areas of brain damage sustained during accidents. It made for gruesome study. On the bright side I became aware of how resilient the brain is when Elsie directed us to studies in which a person's brain had suffered severe injury and the person was able to function more or less normally with only specific areas of disability.

Until the late seventies, psychological testing was the main way in which damage to the brain was revealed. The advent of CAT scans and MRI scans reduced the diagnostic aspect of psychological testing for brain damage and the emphasis moved more to demonstrating the functional impact of damage already established by brain scans.

At the Maudsley hospital in the seventies I assisted in some of those studies by assessing the damage caused by temporal lobe section designed to reduce the impact of severe epilepsy.

Like many psychologists, until 1980 a sizable chunk of my private practice was devoted to demonstrating whether or not brain damage had occurred. After 1980 it was much more likely for referrals of this type to have brain damage already documented by brain scan and psychological testing was requested to determine how this had affected a patient's functioning.

When I worked in private practice I found Elsie's training in neuropsychological testing was invaluable. I was referred a number of people with traumatic brain injury to determine the type and extent of their cognitive disability.

The most memorable of these clients was a man who had suffered a high speed, head-on collision with a concrete bridge plinth in the early seventies. He was taken to a country hospital where a junior surgeon receiving instructions by telephone had repaired the base of his patient's skull. The operation involved removing the top of his skull and folding back the brain in order to carry out the repair to the base of the brain pan, before replacing the brain and the top of the skull.

Sitting in my office reading his hospital file some years later I fully expected my client to arrive by ambulance and wheel chair. To my surprise he arrived by car and walked in. His cognitive disabilities were widespread and he had a much reduced ability to organise himself but he had returned to work in his father's firm with close monitoring. The brain is a marvellously resilient organ.

Elsie's lectures were made more appealing and informative by her remarkably varied interests and background and her enthusiasm for continuing to expand her knowledge in many areas. She had an academic background in the classics – an interest she maintained all her life - and started teaching psychology when she became a junior lecturer at Queensland University in 1937. She was with the psychology Department from its earliest beginnings and during the war she extended her interest in clinical psychology and joined the Volunteer Emergency Psychological Service dealing with psychologically injured returned servicemen and problem recruits.

By the time I became a student in the department in 1962 Elsie was a senior lecturer and had carried the entire clinical offering of the department for some years. About the time I graduated with a PhD eight years later she was a Reader. Such was her impact on psychology that by the end of her career in the 1980s she had been showered with honours ranging from the Order of Australia to an honorary Doctor of Science.

Link
Dr Elsie Harwood
https://www.uq.edu.au/news/article/2006/01/vale-remarkable-dr-elsie-harwood

CHAPTER 29

Test practice and mislaying a client at Goodna

Elsie Harwood's requirement that students learning test administration conduct a large number of practice test administrations on friends and family could and did present the occasional ethical dilemma, which Elsie warned us about several times. Since practice tests are conducted by inexperienced testers there could well be undetected mistakes in administration. As a result it isn't possible to be sure that the results are a valid reflection of the practice subject's cognitive functioning. It would therefore be improper for the test results to be communicated to the subject and most unwise for any life decisions to be based on them.

My test subjects raised no objections to this withholding of test results. Even though some of them had devoted many hours to assisting me none of them pressed me for the results. However, I had my own ethical struggle about one practice subject who I knew quite well. He had twice failed the second year of a three-year degree and was determined to keep trying until he succeeded. His WAIS results indicated that he did not have the intellectual capacity to tackle a degree. For days I struggled with the temptation to let him know that he would never succeed and should devote his energies to something he was more likely to succeed at.

Fortunately I did not tell him. It took him several more years to complete the final years of his degree and subsequently he had a satisfying career in his chosen religious calling. This was a great lesson for me in emphasising that intelligence is not the only factor determining success and in trusting in the wisdom of ethical restrictions. It stood me in good stead when advising my own students who were navigating the same dilemma.

The final stage of WAIS training with Elsie Harwood was combined with my first exposure to a real clinical patient. For me his was no toe in the water session with a mildly anxious patient. I was sent as a mildly anxious psychology student to Goodna (officially the Brisbane Special Hospital) to test a seriously deteriorated patient.

In the nineteen sixties, before the Mental Health Act reforms of 1974 and 2000, Goodna was a huge psychiatric hospital where you could be incarcerated for life by a family doctor at the instigation of a caring (or hostile) family member. Goodna was a name that sent shivers down the spine.

Fortunately the reality was a little better than I expected. Even though the hospital reputedly had more that 2000 patients it seemed completely deserted. The vast acreage of the grounds was well cared for if somewhat depressing - the typical drab brown of a south-east Queensland late-winter lawn as far as the eye could see. Deposited on it in more or less neat rows was a sizeable array of identical fibro huts, each with a small ward number attached, some with a narrow garden running down one side. The huts were painted an identical scaly white, giving the whole place the look and atmosphere of an abandoned army camp. It was very easy to get lost – as I later discovered to my chagrin.

I presented myself at the appropriate ward and was shown down a drab corridor to a windowless room with dark brown polished floorboards and unrelieved white ceiling and walls. There was a desk and two chairs. Otherwise the room was completely bare.

I settled myself in – took the seat behind the desk opposite the door, set up my test materials and waited for my patient about whom I had been told nothing. A lesson well learned that afternoon: never again did I allow myself to be put in the position of testing a patient about whom I knew nothing – especially why they had been referred for testing.

At first impression my patient seemed like an ordinary looking man in hospital garb, around fifty years old, perhaps slightly undernourished. He had an air of deference that I later came to associate with institutionalisation. We chatted for a while, partly to establish rapport, partly to get some background. He had no more idea than I had as to why he had been referred to me. So we got on with the testing.

His conversational style and his answers to the *verbal* items led me to think that he was reasonably bright. It was only towards the end of the session that I developed a suspicion that some of his non-verbal (i.e. visual) subtest scores were quite low. It was hard to be sure because the raw scores need to be converted to standard scores before a proper comparison can be made. I wondered if a problem with visual-spatial reasoning was the reason he had been referred.

We were nearly at the end of the testing session when my patient declared he had an urgent need to go to the toilet. Earlier as I had come along the corridor

I had noticed the gents toilet door almost opposite this room. So without thinking much about the consequences I showed him the toilet door and asked him to return as soon as he had relieved himself. I left the office door open so that it would be easy for him to find me and returned to my seat.

I was quite intrigued by what the test results might show for this man so with nothing else to do for the moment I started to analyse the results. I soon discovered that there was a large discrepancy between his verbal and visual skills. It took a few minutes longer to fully realise the implications of this result. This was a man who could appear to function quite normally verbally, but would struggle with tasks involving spatial perception. Finding his way back to the test room from the toilet could be one of those tasks.

It had been five or ten minutes since I had seen him enter the toilet. More than enough time to relieve himself and return. With a sinking heart I checked the toilet and then the corridor, then the area outside the hut. He had vanished. I had mislaid my first ever patient.

When I nervously reported my patient's absence to the nurse on duty he was somewhat offhand I thought. "Don't worry, he'll turn up. He can't get far. He quite often does this – well known for it. Someone will recognise him and take him back to his ward."

The report for this client was not easy to write up – while the results were remarkable and straightforward to interpret, the section on behavioural observations and the explanation of the missing final subtest score stretched to the limit my ability to report accurately while not embarrassing myself.

Bibliography

Finnane, M. (2008). Wolston Park Hospital, 1865–2001: A Retrospect. *Queensland Review,* 15(2).

Mental Health Act 2000 (Qld). Retrieved from
https://www.legislation.qld.gov.au/LEGISLTN/CURRENT/M/MentalHealthA00.pdf

CHAPTER 30

Elsie Harwood, clinical training and Operation Retirement.

During the time I studied with Elsie she and Dr George Naylor and later Lex Irvine embarked on Operation Retirement, which eventually became a groundbreaking twenty-year study of cognitive functioning during aging. It started from Elsie's conviction that the then current view of cognitive decline with aging was wrong. She was convinced that the idea that older people cannot learn new skills was fundamentally flawed. She chose a rather challenging way to test her contention. In those days it was common knowledge that it was almost impossible to learn a new language after the age of seven and certainly older people would be totally unable to do it. So Elsie set out to teach retirees German.

She is famously quoted as telling older people: *in Germany babies learn to speak German.* So why shouldn't older people in Brisbane be just as successful?

This initial project was so successful that it attracted international interest and funding and became the longest-running, best-known and most influential study on cognitive functioning in aging. It could be argued that Elsie Harwood and Operation Retirement singlehandedly changed the view of cognitive functioning in aging. It is certainly true that older people owe a lot to her insight and persistence in demonstrating that older brains can achieve impressive things.

The University of the Third Age (U3A), which started in Europe at around the same time as Operation Retirement, is a worldwide education movement where both the teachers and the students are older people. The idea that older people are learners and it is good for older people to learn new things owes much to Elsie's research, which is often cited in U3A literature. In Australia the U3A teachers are volunteers and the classes are free – although there is a small membership fee.

In Elsie's clinical courses there was very little instruction in therapeutic technique and almost no patient contact. Most of the practice we had with testing was on each other or on practice subjects, most of whom were subjected to an initially stumbling but gradually more polished rendition of the Wechsler Adult Intelligence Scale (WAIS) – still the most widely used test of cognitive ability.

By today's standards, when it is possible to obtain a PhD in clinical psychology at most Australian universities, this might be seen as an inadequate preparation for a career in clinical psychology, but in Australia in the 1960's it was among the best. It might be argued that it is quite a lot better than the training that is offered to undergraduate psychologists today.

These days most psychologists move into the workforce with an honours degree but most of the clinical training has now been moved to the postgraduate level. As a result most psychologists today do not receive any clinical training before they start work.

A common complaint in the clinical workplace is that compared with other health professionals recently graduated psychologists are not work-ready. Newly graduated psychologists need quite extensive on-the-job training and supervision before they are able to work solo. The difference between psychologists and other professions is that currently in Australia four-year psychology graduates usually have no clinical training. By comparison in the sixties we had the equivalent of two full-year courses in clinical psychology by the time we graduated from the University of Queensland.

These days university psychology departments subscribe to the view that clinical training should be at the post-graduate level and they reserve clinical training for Masters and PhD level students. Universities turn a blind eye to the fact that most psychologists train only to the fourth year level and arrive in the workplace with little clinical training. It is left to psychology registration boards to ensure that psychologists get some extra training, which they do by making registration as a new psychologist contingent on receiving carefully structured supervision in the first two years of employment.

It could be argued that, as a result, the clinical training of the majority of psychologists in Australia (who are four-year trained) has declined significantly over the last 50 years. On the other hand, the elite few who can access the funds and have high enough marks to enrol in a higher degree are quite well prepared for the workplace. They are perhaps not so happy with the starting salary they receive after undergoing six to eight years of training, which, in Queensland, is usually the same salary as four-year trained psychologists.

Certainly the superior training I received from Elsie Harwood set me up for a successful career in clinical psychology, which included a number of years teaching the subject at University level and culminated in the position of Director of Psychology for a large health district. Of course I built on the foundation Elsie provided by undertaking further training over many years, but Elsie's teaching in the sixties formed the basis of my approach to clinical psychology.

Bibliography

Browning, C. & Stacey, B. (1999). Psychology and ageing in Australia. *Australian Psychologist,* 34, 79-81.

Harwood, E. & Enticknap, L. E. (1984). Longitudinal Study Of Intelligence: The Sixteenth Year In "Operation Retirement". *Australian Journal on Ageing,* 3(3), 20–22,

Harwood, E. & Naylor, G. F. K. (1969). Recall and recognition in elderly and young subjects. *Australian Journal of Psychology,* 21, 251-257.

Naylor, G. F. & Harwood, E. (1975). *Old dogs, new tricks. Psychology Today,* 1, 29-33.

CHAPTER 31

Elsie Harwood and Psychological Testing

In the sixties the University of Queensland psychology department produced two face-to-face intelligence tests: the Queensland Test (QT) and the Naylor Harwood Adult Intelligence Scale (NHAIS).

The Naylor Harwood Adult Intelligence Scale (NHAIS) was developed by Elsie Harwood and George Naylor and was probably initially linked to Operation Retirement to provide a way of repeat testing of cognitive functioning.

The NHAIS was designed as a parallel test to the WAIS – the most commonly used intelligence test – which was well known to be contaminated by practice effect. That is: on second and subsequent testing people often obtain a higher score simply because they are more familiar with the test. This presents a problem if you want to test people a number of times, as Elsie wished to do for operation retirement. One solution to this is to split a test in two and use alternate items on the second testing. A more elegant solution is to develop a parallel test.

This Elsie and George did with a masterly technique. Each item of the NHAIS was linked to an item in the WAIS by testing it on a few hundred subjects to make sure it was of equivalent difficulty. Thus the NHAIS can be truly said to be parallel to the WAIS. As a result the NHAIS did not have to be normed so this procedure also saved significant time and resources that would otherwise have been needed to test many thousands of subjects in a norming sample.

During my career I have had several occasions to be grateful for the existence of the NHAIS when I had a need to ascertain the cognitive functioning of someone who was already familiar with the WAIS.

The most notable of these was during the eighties when I was suffering from a severe case of Ross River Fever, which eventually morphed into Myalgic

Encephalomyelitis (now known as Chronic Fatigue Syndrome). To assist in my recovery I was keen to find out as much as I could about the disorder, how it was affecting me and in particular how to recover from it. To do this I spent several months as a daily visitor to the Herston Medical Library in Brisbane reading and photocopying every scientific publication about it that I could find.

I was aware that I was experiencing some cognitive problems – mostly with memory, attention, processing speed and visual spatial ability. I found in the scientific literature some inconclusive references to this sort of cognitive deficit in CFS patients. Naturally I was keen to know exactly what impact the disorder had on my own cognitive functioning.

I was very familiar with the WAIS after years of practice in its use so it would not be possible to get an accurate assessment of my cognitive functioning from that test. On the other hand I had only once looked at the NHAIS some years before, so I was as uncontaminated by practice effect as a psychologist could be. A colleague who was familiar with this test was able to administer it to me.

As predicted, while my overall IQ seemed reasonably unaffected, my visual- spatial, and memory scores were depressed as were those requiring attention and processing speed.

Recent studies with CFS patients have confirmed difficulty with memory, attention and processing speed (Shanks *et al* 2013, DeLuca 2000). The problem I had (and still have) with visual-spatial tasks seems to be unique to me and may have predated the CFS and been exacerbated by the illness perhaps.

Knowing this about my cognitive functioning helped a great deal with my self-directed rehabilitation from CFS. Armed with these results I was better able to predict what activities I could accomplish with my usual skill level and what was likely to give me trouble. As a result I could focus my efforts on things I could succeed in, and rehearse or find alternative ways of doing things that I found difficult – or simply avoid them.

Years later my processing speed is still slower than I would like it to be and I have occasional lapses of attention. In other words I am slower in thinking on my feet. I still find myself avoiding the use of visual memory and rely as much as I can on verbal memory and kinaesthetic cues. My ability to get lost without a GPS is legendary.

Of course, as I move into my early seventies, old age has become a convenient explanation for any cognitive problems when other people notice.

In deciding to become very familiar with my illness and study its effects on me I believe I was following an example set by Elsie Harwood. I have been told that Elsie contracted a severe illness in the seventies (possibly encephalitis) and during her recovery kept a diary of the changes she noticed in her cognitive ability. This courageous and scientific approach to adversity is so much like Elsie that I have no hesitation in believing this story. On the other hand I have no concrete confirmation that it is true. If any of my readers has any information that will help to clarify the accuracy of this information I would be grateful if you would let me know.

Regardless of the veracity of this account of Elsie's illness I am sure that my own approach to recovery owed much to my belief that I was following a path pioneered by one of my wisest teachers. The information that I obtained in the medical library was very useful in assisting my medical advisors to devise a treatment program that was well ahead of its time and eventually effective in returning me to a relatively normal lifestyle.

Bibliography

Shanks, L., Jason, L., Evans, M. & Brown, A. (2013). Cognitive impairments associated with CFS and POTS. *Frontiers in Physiology*, 4, 113. Retrieved from http://www.ncbi.nlm.nih.gov/pmc/articles/PMC3655280/

DeLuca, J. (2000). Neurocognitive Impairment in CFS. Retrieved from http://www.anapsid.org/cnd/diagnosis/neurocog.html

CHAPTER 32

Commem week pranks

The 1960s was the zenith of commemoration week pranks. Commem week celebrations had been a tradition since at least the turn of the century and by the sixties the festivities had solidified around a number of customary activities: the graduation ceremony, the parade with floats, political commentary and protest, raising money for charity, ritualised heavy drinking. And pranks.

What started as a fun way of letting off steam morphed into veneration of intelligence and diligence with each element contributing its own essential ingredient.

I regarded the whole thing as an academic religious observance and as with other religious practices I engaged in some with gusto and completely ignored others. Like other religious observances commem week has recently fallen into disuse and has hardly made a ripple since the early eighties except in TV shows like *The Chaser's War on Everything*. It is a sad loss to university life and to the sometimes-troubled relationship between Town and Gown.

In particular I miss the witty daring of commem week pranks the best of which made pointed social comment, such as poking fun at pomposity and fame.

The earliest one I have heard of involved strapping a bra to the Cenotaph in the 1930s. Judging by the extremely negative reaction of the RSL this one must have had deep social resonance at the time.

In 1956 the reception of the Olympic torch was pre-empted by a University student running the last part of the prescribed route and presenting the Lord Mayor of Sydney with a very presentable Olympic torch made of a used fruit tin nailed to a wooden chair leg. It almost fooled the Mayor who approached the microphone to begin his speech just as the real Olympic torchbearer came into view.

One class of engineers carried their unpopular lecturer's Mini Minor into the lecture theatre and balanced it with its front wheels astride the lectern. The lecturer rose to the occasion and repaid the students with a rather boring impromptu lecture on the internal combustion engine. The students had the last laugh. They left the theatre at the end of the lecture, ignoring the lecturer's demands that they return his car to the car park.

One group of students expressed their displeasure at a young man's habit of returning to his college late every Sunday night so drunk and disorderly that he had to crawl along the corridor to his room waking everyone in the process. One Sunday night they bricked up his doorway and allowed him to crawl up and down the corridor looking for his door until he fell asleep on the floor. Then they removed the bricks so that he wasn't able to work out what they had done.

In 1964 on the eve of the Beatles Australian tour some students put up signs indicating that the tour had been cancelled. The outraged fans jammed the switchboard of the booking agents and theatres.

Other pranks were simply silly and did not really try to make a point such as putting dye in fountains, having Gough Whitlam launch a bed-wetting competition or running treasure hunts requiring participants to bring to the campus unusual items such as a celebrity's wig, a road grader and a real pink elephant.

A student in a large crowded lecture theatre responded loudly to a call for help on his mobile phone, changed into a superman costume in front of the amazed audience and charged off to render assistance.

Quite a few pranks were dedicated to inventive ways of raising money for charity. Students took to the highways to walk long distances in the silliest fashion possible. They pushed scooters from Melbourne to Sydney and wheeled a keg of beer in a baby's pram from Sydney to Wollongong to raise money for charity. Students attempted to set a record for how many people could squeeze into a mobile toilet to raise money for a charitable cause.

Students kidnapped people and valuables to ransom them for charity. Normie Rowe's supporters paid up handsomely as did a Townsville radio station for the return of their most popular DJ.

Perhaps the most outrageous of these charitable money-raising attempts was the kidnapping of the judge's seat from one of the higher courts in Townsville. This was a very special chair modelled on the English throne complete with a large stone under the seat and was said to be very dear to the presiding judge. It was considered to be well worth capturing and the college boys who carried out the heist expected to raise a large sum with its ransom.

Each year the two main residential colleges in Townsville were in fierce competition to see who could raise the most money, so when the opposing college heard of the judges chair coup they were determined to come up with a plan to raise even more money. After several days when they still did not have a viable plan they decided on a desperate scheme to steal the chair from the opposing college and ransom it themselves.

The plan went horribly wrong. They were caught by the opposing college boys in the act of re-stealing the chair just as they were loading it onto a small truck. They had no time to tie it down and in a panic they took off at great speed chased by their rivals. The chair fell off the truck at the first corner. Both groups of college boys surveyed the damage with dismay.

The trail goes cold at that point. I suspect that the rivals may have united in their attempt to avoid being implicated and worse, having to face the ire of the judge – possibly in his own court. Needless to say neither college raised much money that year. I hope the chair was well insured.

Perhaps the best prank I have heard of both in terms of its cleverness and the amount of mayhem it caused for least effort, was carried out by one student making two phone calls. The provenance of this prank is a little obscure. Some say it occurred in Melbourne and some in Sydney. There are also versions of this story originating in New Zealand and America. So the whole episode may be apocryphal, but it is so clever that I must include it.

The prank is this: workers were digging up the road outside the University; a student rang the police and complained that students masquerading as council workers were digging up the road.

It is already a funny prank, but now the extra twist.

The student then rang the Council and complained that students dressed as police are interfering with council workers engaged in road work outside the University.

Mayhem ensued as police and council workers arrived en masse and accused each other of being university students.

Why is that prank so appealing? It has elements of anti-authoritarianism; it is funny; it is clever; no one gets caught; no one gets hurt and above all it takes very little effort. The ideal prank.

Bibliography

The Sixties, (2009). Illawarra Unity, 9(1) Retrieved from
http://ro.uow.edu.au/cgi/viewcontent.cgi?article=1131&context=unity

Pranks, Silliness and General Tomfoolery, (n.d.). Sydney University Comedy Society. Retrieved from
http://comedysoc.com/history.html

Bridge over Parramatta Road. (2008, November 1), Sydney morning herald. Retrieved from http://www.smh.com.au/news/national/bridge-over-parramatta-road/2008/01/10/1199554833030.html

Robinson, S. & Ustinoff, J. (Eds.). (2012). The 1960s in Australia: People, Power and Politics. Cambridge: Cambridge Scholars Publishing.

CHAPTER 33

Further adventures in testing

In the sixties the University of Queensland psychology department produced two face-to-face intelligence tests: the Queensland Test (QT) and the Naylor Harwood Adult Intelligence Scale (NHAIS). Considering the enormous amount of work that is required, and the small size of the staff, this achievement speaks volumes for the energy and vitality of the department.

To produce an intelligence test first requires the invention, production and refinement of lots of individual items and then a study to determine their level of difficulty, which involves an individual trial administration to hundreds of subjects. Following that the test is standardised by individual administration to a large number of test subjects carefully selected to represent the age, sex and socioe-conomic groups the test is intended for.

This process involves years of work by a dedicated team before the huge effort involved in publishing and marketing. That the fledgling psychology department at Queensland University managed this feat twice in less than ten years is remarkable.

I became aware of the Queensland Test in 1965 when I was in my fourth year at University and volunteered to assist in testing a norming sample at the Dunwich State School. I was selected to join the team based on my having passed Dr Elsie Harwood's test administration exam and my willingness to take a long bus and ferry ride to Dunwich and to camp for a week with other testers in a set of huts. I seem to recall that we were all paid too.

In a class outing atmosphere we settled into the huts, which seemed to be of Second World War vintage – or possibly earlier. They were designed for a communal lifestyle with dormitory style sleeping accommodation and shared ablutions.

I was fascinated to see my male colleagues shaving in the communal bathroom. About that time I decided not to shave and I was intrigued by those who had decided to continue with this daily torture. Not shaving has been one of my enduring life decisions, partly because I find it painful and partly because it seems like an odd affectation to remove hair from one part of the head. I now realise that I was travelling against the trend on this issue. These days people remove hair not only from the face, top and sides of the head but also from more intimate parts of the body. As I get older I am losing more and more hair from the top of my head but apparently this also is not fashionable.

But I digress.

I enjoyed the sense of community that resulted from living and working closely with people I had previously only rubbed shoulders with in the classroom. Of course we were all very determined to have a good time.

After a week or so of testing all day in a classroom at Dunwich School we returned to the University to analyse the results. It did not seem like the hard work that it really was – more like an extended practical class in a holiday camp.

Dunwich is located on North Stradbroke Island off the coast of Queensland a little way south of Brisbane and is notable for the size of its Aboriginal population – the main reason this school was selected as a norming site.

The Queensland Test (QT) was developed by McElwain and Kearney and published in 1970. It was based on previous test batteries, in particular the Pacific Islands Regiment Test (PIRT), which was designed to select candidates for the Pacific Islands Regiment (Ord, 1968). For the Queensland Test the materials were substantially modified to suit modern Australian testing conditions. In particular the materials were smaller and made of colourful plastic (still a novelty in the early sixties) rather that wood. This considerably reduced the weight and size of the test kit. Whereas the PIRT was transported in a crate, the QT could be tucked under the psychologists arm in a small briefcase sized test kit.

The attractiveness of the items, the happy group of testers and the isolation of a semi-tropical island gave the whole experience an otherworldly quality, which I remember with some fondness.

The QT was designed to be non-verbal so the instructions had to be delivered non-verbally using demonstration and gesture to instruct and encourage the children performing the test. This requirement and the fact that this was the first time I had come into contact with a sizable group of Aboriginal children added to the otherworldly ambience.

As well as patiently bearing with us - a strange group of young white adults who pretended not to be able to speak to children - these children were remarkably generous in allowing us to be momentarily part of their lives. One group showed us how to catch birds for tea after school. Their technique was based on the observation that galahs feeding in the top of a large tree would swoop quite low when transferring as a flock to a nearby tree. The children would stand in the flight path with rocks and sticks held behind their backs and call and whistle to the birds to encourage them to fly down. When they did the birds were met with a hail of missiles which felled one more often than not. They were quite merciless in killing these birds and proudly carried them off home for tea.

Many years later I would rediscover this ingenuous quality when working with Aboriginal groups in the central desert region of Australia. While the adults were gracious and persistent in teaching vocabulary, language structure, connection to the land, dreaming stories and polite behaviour, the children boisterously enjoyed teaching slang and swear words and would loudly chant their latest offering with gales of infectious laughter. It was thanks to these children that I was able to give an exaggerated impression of my facility with the desert languages by being able to swear fluently in a number of them.

The atmosphere of unreality I experienced in my first encounter with a group of Aborigines at Dunwich returned every time I spent time with Aboriginal groups on their home ground. Besides the culture being so different from my own, their recent history and mine diverged so much that I had to continually adjust my worldview to accommodate their experience.

For example: at Cundeelee in Western Australia in the early eighties I was told how the Pila Nguru (the Spinifex People) had been rounded up at gunpoint in the sixties – a little over ten years before. I was so shocked that I interrupted an elder's discourse with my amazement and dismay. After a few moments he said kindly "OK, forget about guns" and continued with his recent history.

I had to continually remind myself that these kind, polite people belong to the land I was in and I was a visitor. It seemed that I was being constantly steered to safety through a social and religious minefield of potential faux pas and sacrilege. This sense of divergent world view is epitomised by the striking, humorous graffiti at the Alice Springs airport in the eighties – also noted by Salman Rushdie in his autobiography – *Surrender white man, your town is surrounded.*

Bibliography

Cane, S. (2002). *PILA NGURU: The Spinifex People,* Freemantle: Fremantle Arts Centre Press .

McElwain, D. W. & Kearney, G. E. (1970). *Queensland test handbook : a test of general cognitive ability designed for use under conditions of reduced communication.* Hawthorn, Vic: Australian Council for Educational Research.

McElwain, D. W. & Kearney, G. E. (1973). Intellectual development. In G. E. Kearney, P. R. de Lacey & G. R. Davidson (Eds.), *The psychology of Aboriginal Australians.* (pp. 43- 56). Sydney: John Wiley & Sons Australasia.

Ord, I.G. (1968). The PIR test and its derivatives. *Australian Psychologist*, 2, 137-146.

Ord. I. G. (1971). Assessing the cognitive capacities of non-literate New Guinea adults [monograph supplement]. *New Guinea Psychologist*, 23.

Rickwood, D., Dudgeon, P., & Gridley, H. (2010) A History of Psychology in Aboriginal and Torres Strait Islander Mental Health. In Purdie, N., Dudgeon, P., & Walker, R. (Eds.), *Working Together: Aboriginal and Torres Strait Islander Mental Health and Wellbeing Principles and Practice.* Commonwealth of Australia: Department of Health and Ageing. Retrieved from http://aboriginal.telethonkids.org.au/media/54856/part_1_chapter2.pdf

Rushdie, Salman. (2012). *Joseph Anton: A Memoir.* New York: Random House.

CHAPTER 34

The Queensland Test and Cultural Fairness

I was very fortunate to have early experience in using the Queensland Test during its norming phase and the experience came in very handy at several points in my career when diagnosing Aboriginal clients.

When working with the Central Australian Aboriginal Legal Aid Service in the eighties I was asked to assess the IQ of a deaf traditional Aboriginal adult – a task that would have been well nigh impossible without the Queensland Test.

In the seventies I used the QT when I was asked to give an opinion as to whether a bright Aboriginal adolescent from a mission in Far North Queensland would thrive or fail if sent to Brisbane for the final years of schooling. Quite apart from the effects of disruption and culture shock the teachers had raised the question of whether "bright" in Far North Queensland translates to "bright" in Brisbane – there being a widely held view that children from isolated areas of the bush do not do as well in school as children from the city.

The Queensland Test norms provide evidence that indigenous people who live further from European centres of population do have lower IQ scores. McElwain and Kearney (1973) concluded that

the Aboriginal groups are inferior to Europeans, and in approximately the same degree as they have lacked contact with European groups ... It seems clear that test results are dependent to a considerable degree upon contact or some variable related to contact (p. 47).

Speculation about the reason that Aboriginal and other non-European groups score less on European IQ tests has been a thorny issue for psychologists. Some have argued that the lower IQ score is an indication of racial inferiority (e.g. Fraser, 1995; Herrnstein and Murray, 1994). Others have argued that race is an inaccurate and outmoded concept and IQ tests are by their very nature racist because they lend strength to such arguments (e.g. Better, 2008).

The above quote from McElwain and Kearney indicates that the authors of the QT do not subscribe to the view that racial inferiority explains their results. From my own experience working alongside these two psychologists over a number of years I can confirm that neither of them had sympathy with racist views.

But the mystery of the lower IQ scores on the QT for tribal Aborigines seems to have remained.

A possible explanation is that removing verbal content did not go far enough to make the QT *culture fair*. The puzzles used to test for intelligence in the QT are all of European origin. They are almost exclusively based on geometric shapes and puzzles far more familiar to Europeans than hunter-gatherer indigenes. They are based on an essentially European idea of *clever*.

After spending some time with traditional Aboriginal groups in remote Australia it gradually dawned on me that Aborigines might have quite a different idea of what constitutes *clever*. Aboriginal people might for example value the ability to locate water holes or remember the extremely complex kinship system that influences most indigenous social interactions. Skill in tracking and being able to read sign language at a distance might also be important signs of *cleverness*. If a traditional Aborigine were to create items for an intelligence test it would probably include these and other skills important to a traditional Aboriginal way of life.

Needless to say city-based Europeans would probably not do as well as indigenous hunter-gatherers on such a test. And it is likely that the European's score would improve with proximity to and experience with the hunter-gatherer way of life.

I think it would be very difficult – perhaps impossible - for a European to develop IQ test items based on an Aboriginal concept of cleverness. It might be possible to ask a traditional Aborigine to devise such items but whether that would result in an IQ test, as Europeans understand the term, is an open question.

If this is true then perhaps it is impossible to produce a *culture fair* IQ test. It might be possible to produce an IQ test, which is fairer to Aborigines, based on an Aboriginal definition of cleverness as I have suggested, but such a test would very likely be unfair to members of other cultures.

It seems likely to me that intelligence is expressed through a cultural medium and it may turn out to be impossible to produce one test that correctly and comparably measures the IQ of people regardless of culture.

Nevertheless the QT has been an important clinical tool for me and I'm sure for many other psychologists. The provision of norms for various groups of

Aborigines with various levels of European contact has enabled clinical decisions to made with a far greater accuracy than was previously possible.

In 2016 the Australian Psychological Society (APS) recognised the importance of the issues raised here in its formal apology to Aboriginal and Torres Strait Islander Australians. The apology directly addresses the issue of inappropriate use and interpretation of psychological tests and among other things apologises for:

The inappropriate use of assessment techniques and procedures that have conveyed misleading and inaccurate messages about the abilities and capacities of Aboriginal and Torres Strait Islander people.

The APS apology paves the way for examining the issues from a perspective fully shared with indigenous participants, and hopefully will pave the way to resolving some of the serious issues of cultural fairness in intellectual assessments.

Bibliography

Better, Shirley. (2008). Institutional Racism: A Primer on Theory and Strategies for Social Change. Plymouth, UK: Rowman & Littlefield

Herrnstein, Richard J. & Murray, Charles. (1994). The Bell Curve: Intelligence and Class Structure in American Life. New York: Free Press.

Fraser, S. (1995). The bell curve wars: Race, intelligence, and the future of America. New York: Harper Collins.

McElwain, D. W. & Kearney, G. E. (1970). Queensland Test Handbook : A test of general cognitive ability designed for use under conditions of reduced communication. Hawthorn, Vic: Australian Council for Educational Research.

McElwain, D. W. & Kearney, G. E. (1973. Intellectual Development. In G. E. Kearney, P. R. de Lacey & G. R. Davidson (Eds.), The Psychology of Aboriginal Australians (pp43-56). Sydney: John Wiley.

Westerman, T. & Wettinger, M. (1997). Psychological assessment and intervention. Psychologically Speaking. Retrieved from https://eyeriscreations.com/ips/wp-content/uploads/2016/11/Psychological-Assessment-of-Aboriginal-People.pdf

Links

Apology to Aboriginal and Torres Strait Islander Peoplefrom the Australian Psychological Societydelivered by Professor Tim Careyat the Australian Psychological Society Congress - 15 September 2016.
http://www.psychology.org.au/news/media_releases/15September2016/

CHAPTER 35

Critical decisions

My honours year was a year of critical decisions that would shape my life for many years. In the personal sphere I proposed to my girlfriend and we agreed to marry as soon as I graduated. The decision was easy – I was deeply in love. I had no intention of failing my honours year.

The academic sphere presented a more complicated decision: what sort of psychologist did I want to be? The topics I chose for my research theses would determine the direction that my career would take. I was sharply conscious that the Psychology Department's values and my personal aspirations were not well aligned. The Queensland University Psychology Department (along with most other psychology departments in Australia) was strongly geared to academic, scientific psychology. My personal preference was strongly leaning towards clinical and practical psychology.

It may seem odd from the perspective of this century that clinical research would be considered so unscientific that a thesis in that area would almost certainly be considered to be of low standard regardless of its actual scientific merit. Unfortunately that was the prejudice of the times and echoes of it still linger on in some academic psychology departments.

My personal history had a strong influence on why I was inclined to risk a clinical thesis. When I was 6 years old, during a long stay in hospital during which my parents were not allowed to visit, at some point I decided to be a doctor and devote my life to healing others. That aspiration developed and grew in me over the years despite sincere advice from my teachers that my poor academic results and erratic coordination did not suit me to such an exalted profession.

I worked in a butcher's shop for the summer holidays when I was 16 and I found the sight of blood and raw meat was very disturbing. On reflection I reluctantly decided that embarking on a career involving considerable exposure to other peoples blood and guts would be a serious mistake.

And now six years after that dream-shattering realisation it felt like redemption to realise I could become a healer after all – by a different route. It was too good a chance to pass up.

In one of life's little ironies I later successfully completed a PhD, so I also became a doctor – by a different route.

Jung (1945) was among the first of the modern era to popularise the idea of the *wounded healer*. More recently research by Barr (2006) indicates that more than 70% of counsellors and psychotherapists *have experienced one or more wounding experiences leading to career choice.*

So it is no unusual coincidence that my early experience in hospital, combined with other traumatic experiences in my early life (I was born in London in the middle of the second world war) led me to career choices that resulted in my becoming a clinical psychologist.

In part the choice of psychology was due the narrow range of choices. At University of Queensland in the early sixties there was not a lot of choice of healing professions to train in. University courses in occupational therapy, speech therapy and physiotherapy did not start until the mid to late sixties. I flirted with social work and psychology for a couple of years and in the end decided on psychology.

I have to say that my mother was also influential in my choice of profession. She really liked the idea of psychology and became a psychologist herself later. She sat with me while I filled in the enrolment form for my first year to make sure that I made the right choices.

Against my personal inclination to devote my life to healing psychology was the prejudice of the times that a clinical thesis would automatically be considered of low quality. All things considered, this was not an unreasonable prejudice. In Australia the profession of psychology had only recently separated itself from philosophy on the grounds that psychology was a science based on empirical and experimental methodology, whereas philosophy was based on logic, theory and argument. At that time many clinical publications were generally of a philosophical nature – arguing mainly from the point of view of theory based on logic rather than data. Publications in other areas such as perception and learning were more often based on replicable scientific experimentation. As a result there was a widespread notion that studies in perception and learning were scientific whereas those in the clinical area were not. And from this derived the idea that clinical studies were of lesser quality in a scientific discipline.

So my dilemma was: do I prepare a thesis on a clinical topic and face the possibility of not doing well in, or even not passing, my fourth year; or should I prepare a thesis on a perceptual phenomenon and risk derailing my prospects of becoming a clinical psychologist.

I risked a compromise. The department required two theses at the fourth year level. I decided to submit a perception experiment for the major thesis and a clinical investigation for the minor thesis. I hoped that in this way I could keep a foot in both camps and not risk failing my honours year.

My impression that a clinical thesis would be regarded as being of lower quality was confirmed a year later when discussing the direction my PhD thesis investigation should take. My head of department, Professor McElwain, dismissed out of hand my secondary honours thesis on the analysis of dream content and advised me to focus on the subject of my primary honours thesis – an explanation for the autokinetic illusion – the apparent movement of a pinpoint of light observed in complete darkness.

Although this illusion had been studied for over 100 years there was no explanation for why it occurred. It sparked my interest because it was a problem during the Second World War when pilots flew in formation in the dark, guided only by small lights on the wing tips of other planes.

It was thought that a number of aircraft accidents had been caused by the autokinetic illusion. Pilots flying in formation at night reacted as though another plane had moved closer when in fact it had not. It was thought that, guided only by a tiny, apparently moving light, the pilots had suddenly swerved and had flown into the path of another plane in the formation. A number of other publications indicated that the autokinetic illusion was a problem in other circumstances where people were required to operate in the dark.

I was interested to find out if the illusion occurred in other senses. I reasoned that if the illusion only occurred in vision then the explanation for why an isolated stationary light appeared to move would be in the way the eyes operated. If the illusion occurred with hearing and other senses then the explanation would be a more general one concerning the way the brain receives and processes information from all the senses.

I decided to try auditory location, kinaesthetic (body position), and heat location in addition to the usual visual illusion. I was allocated a laboratory on the lower ground floor of the Social Sciences building and got to work

Bibliography

Barr, A. (2006). An Investigation Into The Extent To Which Psychological Wounds Inspire Counsellors And Psychotherapists To Become Wounded Healers, The Significance Of These Wounds On Their Career Choice, The Causes Of These Wounds And The Overall Significance Of Demographic Factors. (Unpublished masters thesis). University of Strathclyde. Abstract retrieved from https://issuu.com/imran_manzoor/docs/wounded_healer_research_alison_barr_part_1_of_2
Also appears as a paper presented at COSCA Research Dialogue. Abstract retrieved from http://www.thegreenrooms.net/wounded-healer/ Full copy available from alison@thegreenrooms.net

Freud, S. (1933). Notes on a case of obsessional neurosis, In *Collected Papers*, Vol III, pp 149-295. Hogarth press: London.

Groesbeck, C. (1975). The Archetypal Image of the Wounded Healer. *Journal of Analytical Psychology*, 20(2), 122–145.

Wolgien, C. & Coady, N. (1997). Good Therapists' Beliefs About the Development of Their Helping Ability: The Wounded Healer Paradigm Revisited. *The Clinical Supervisor,* 15(2).

CHAPTER 36

The autokinetic illusion and dreams

Even though I had made it clear that my autokinetic illusion (AKI) experiment would be conducted in the dark, the laboratory I was allocated had an entire wall of floor to ceiling sliding glass windows (and an excellent view across the sports fields to the Brisbane River). Even with heavy blackout curtains and several hundred yards of gaffer tape it was still possible to see across the room after a few minutes of dark adaption. For the AKI to occur four times (visual, auditory, heat and kinaesthetic) I needed complete darkness for around 30 minutes.

Ingenuity (I'm not sure if it was mine or the skilled and helpful technician's) came to the rescue. Not for nothing was this era of psychological experimentation referred to as *sticky tape and string*. We used several rolls of gaffer tape, black paint on cardboard and more, heavier blackout curtains before I declared myself beaten by daylight. The blackout was not effective for more than a few minutes, so I decided to blindfold the subjects as well.

After much trial and error I arrived at a procedure that I described in my write-up as: *Subjects were blindfolded with an opaque diver's mask and led into the laboratory...*

Leading blindfolded first year students into an almost completely darkened room was great fun and led inevitably to some interesting and hilarious episodes that were not reported in my write up.

After they were seated subjects were asked to report on the position of a pure tone, a heated one bar radiator, a fixed vertical rod held at arms length and a pinpoint of light; one after the other. Of course the pinpoint of light could not be seen through the mask so my subjects were asked to close their eyes and change masks. The second mask was set in the end of a black tube made out of a discarded inside tube of a massive roll of paper, rather like an enormous toilet roll insert. It was enclosed at the far end and painted black inside and out. The pinpoint of light was made by pricking the far end of the tube with a pin. It was literally a pinpoint.

A jungle of laboratory stands, stools and chin rests (and of course lots of gaffer tape) were used to set this all up in such a way that I could find my way through it in the dark and seat my subjects without injuring anyone and then give the instructions and record responses. I learned to write in the dark. Unsurprisingly my handwriting did not differ much from my usual illegible scrawl.

I was intrigued and delighted to find that almost everybody reported movement of all the stationary stimuli. So I could report that the autokinetic illusion occurred in hearing, heat sensitivity and kinaesthesia (sense of body position) as well as vision.

I was able to draw the conclusion that the autokinetic illusion is more likely to be a function of the way the brain and nervous system operate rather than the way that the eyes operate.

My secondary thesis – the clinical one that I was really interested in - was an attempt to give a scientific basis to dream work.

When choosing this topic I didn't fully realise that I was venturing into the most disreputable of all the areas of clinical psychology at the time. If clinical work was regarded as unscientific, dream work was at the extreme end of the snake-oil range. I had decided to try to bring some scientific rigour to an area that most 1960s psychologists regarded as hogwash.

One of the big problems in the interpretation of dreams at that time centred on what should be considered normal dreams and what can be described as unusual dreams. Dream theorists and practitioners for example Jung (1956) and Freud (1900) considered that dream symbolism was unusual if they had not encountered it previously in the dreams of other patients. In other words they derived their concept of normal dreams from the dreams of a group of people who were in therapy and by definition not a representative sample of the normal population.

This seemed to me to be a good starting point for the study of dreams – to find out what ordinary people normally dream about. A normative study of dreams collected from ordinary people.

At that time only one study had been published which attempted to do this – a large American study by Hall in 1953. Hall's study involved a large team of researchers copying down dreams verbatim as people told them. My study aimed to try out a more efficient way of collecting dreams and also to see if Americans and Australians dream similar or different dreams.

For my first attempt at this I gave over a hundred adolescents an open-ended questionnaire asking for a list of objects, animals and people occurring in a specific dream, the theme of the dream and the emotion they felt during the dream. The choice of school children was fortuitous in that I was able to persuade the head teacher of my old high school to let me use a few classes of students at my old school as subjects.

The preliminary discussion with my old headmaster was rather bizarre. First we had to work through his surprise and delight that I had made it into university and was now at the fourth year level. Secondly his only concern with the design of my survey was that it should not contain any reference to sex.

I was a little taken aback until I realised that he thought sex was the only thing adolescents dreamed about, and sex was therefore going to be an important part of my study. In that era, before sex education was a standard subject at school, raising the subject of sex (even dreamed sex) would be likely to cause serious concern. I got the feeling that my old headmaster didn't want to be known as the headmaster who was sacked for allowing teenagers to think about sex.

I reassured him that sex did not figure in my survey and showed him my questionnaire, which only asked about themes, objects, animals, people and emotions. The word *Sex* appeared at the top of the page alongside the word *Age*. I reassured him that this referred to the gender of the respondent. He was satisfied and the survey went ahead with no hitches.

The second form of the questionnaire was a tick-and-flick version of the first with a list of categories based on the results of the first questionnaire. This version was given to 50 university students in a classroom setting.

The results showed that my respondents dreamed mostly about vehicles and buildings, pets, parents and friends. The dreams were mostly set in areas similar to the areas in which they lived. Pleasant and unpleasant emotions were reported equally. The majority of the themes of the dreams centered on security, escape and aggression.

In other words the dreams of these young Queenslanders were more or less typical of their day-to-day experience. There was no difference attributable to age or gender.

Interestingly 25% of respondents reported dreams that had a sexual theme. According to Mustanski (2011) this is close to the proportion of time people spend thinking about sex when awake.

There were several differences between my study and Hall's (1953) American study. The most interesting are that Americans tend to dream more about unpleasantness, aggression and sex, while Australians tend to dream more about the outdoors.

Of course the most important finding was that it is possible to meaningfully collect 100 dreams in around 20 minutes rather than the several days it takes using individual transcription.

These days I'm happy to say dream research is a large and fascinating field of scientific study. If you are interested in this field you might find Schneider and Domhoff (2015) useful background reading.

If you are interested in the details of either of my theses they can be accessed at the University of Queensland library.

Bibliography

Freud, S. (1900). *The interpretation of dreams*. London: Hogarth Press.

Hall, C. (1953). *The meaning of dreams*. N.Y: Wiley.

Hills, I. (1965). *Dream Content Analysis* (Unpublished honours thesis). University of Queensland.

Hills, I. (1965). *The Autokinetic effect* (Unpublished honours thesis). University of Queensland.

Jung, C.J. (1956). *Collected works* (Vol. 5). *Symbols of transformation*. London: Routledge and Kegan Paul

Mustanski. B. (2011). *The Sexual Continuum*. Retrieved from https://www.psychologytoday.com/blog/the-sexual-continuum/201112/how-often-do-men-and-women-think-about-sex

Schneider, A. & Dumhoff, G. W. (2015). *The Quantitative Study of Dreams*. Retrieved from http://www.dreamresearch.net/

CHAPTER 37

My first teaching job and the legacy of Moorlands

During my final undergraduate year at Queensland University I was offered a job teaching social and developmental psychology to kindergarten teachers. I need to backtrack a little to explain how that came about.

The reason my family had migrated to Australia six years previously was in order for my mother to take up a position as the principal of the Kindergarten Teachers College.

I'm not sure whether the college was short of a social psychology teacher or whether my mother decided that this job would be good experience for me. Either way it must have been seen as blatant nepotism by the rest of the staff – particularly the resident psychologist. I must say given these circumstances the permanent staff members of the Kindergarten Teacher's College were extremely generous in their acceptance of me.

I should point out that nepotism was *de rigueur* in Queensland at that time and would be for some time to come. Nepotism and conflict of interest could be seen as a hallmark of Queensland politics in the sixties and the rest of Queensland society took its lead from its politicians. For example, a private company of which the Queensland Premier was chairman, was awarded a government contract to build the railway from a coastal port to the inland coal mining areas. In other words the government had awarded a lucrative private contract to its premier minister. When asked to justify this conflict of interest the Premier, Bjelke-Petersen, replied with some impatience:

"What do you want us to do? Give these jobs to people we don't know"?

So in those days it was probably considered to be OK for the principal of a college to employ her son.

After a while I discovered that the college's resident teacher of psychology had no qualifications in psychology so I didn't feel so bad about reducing his workload by a couple of hours a week. In those days there was no registration requirement for psychologists so there was nothing to prevent a person calling themselves a psychologist regardless of their background or lack of a psychology degree. And it seems to be a pattern even today for academics to enter psychology from backgrounds as diverse as history, engineering, divinity and biology.

The Kindergarten Teachers College was at that stage housed in a lovely old Queensland mansion called Moorlands on Coronation Drive. I recall its wonderful sweeping staircase to the second floor, patterned ceilings and wooden floors. There were magnificent views over the lawns to the Brisbane River marred only by the busy Coronation Drive, which hugs the riverbank all the way from the City to Toowong. My classes were conducted in a sumptuously wood-panelled room – probably a large dining room or reception room in its heyday.

Moorlands has an interesting history. It was built and previously lived in by the Mayne family. Anyone who attended Queensland University in the sixties would have heard of the Mayne family who famously donated the land on which the St Lucia campus now stands. Enfolded in a curve of the Brisbane River the University's St Lucia campus is now situated on very expensive prime real estate.

When I left the University in 1969 the construction of the main hall had just started and was named *Mayne Hall* – a slightly quirky play on words that speaks volumes about the sense of humour of the University administrators. The name was changed in 2004 to Mayne Centre to add another layer to the joke and to reflect its repurposing as an art gallery. In the sixties there was even a student song that referred to the University as Maynesland.

So I was very familiar with the name Mayne.

I was at that time less familiar with the darker side of the Mayne family history. According to historian Rosamond Siemon (1997) Patrick Mayne allegedly obtained his start by murdering a timber-getter in the mid-eighteen hundreds and stealing his money. This man had just been paid off and while drinking away some of his earnings in a pub in south Brisbane, was boasting, unwisely as it turned out, about his huge windfall. His body was found dismembered and scattered in various hidey-holes in the area. Patrick Mayne allegedly framed the cook at the Hotel who was subsequently hanged for the murder even though he consistently denied the charge.

Subsequently Patrick bought a butcher's shop for about the same amount that had been stolen from the timber getter and gradually built his fortune by speculating any spare earnings in real estate. He died aged 41, a hugely wealthy but broken man. Reportedly his behaviour had become more and more erratic in his later years and he was eventually confined to the house at Moorlands where he made a deathbed confession to the murder.

The police dismissed this confession on the grounds that he was of unsound mind and such people often confessed on their deathbeds to crimes they had not committed. The population of Brisbane was not totally convinced and it was reported that the huge crowd that turned out to his funeral wanted only to see whether the horses would refuse to draw his hearse. It was a common belief at the time that horses would refuse to pull a hearse containing the body of a murderer. They were not disappointed. According to newspaper reports at the time the horses did refuse to pull the hearse and had to be whipped until the blood ran in order to get them to move.

The story becomes sadder still. Mayne's widow continued to operate the butcher shop. She took over his estate and built the lovely house at Moorlands where she and her adult children lived. Some of the children showed signs of having inherited the father's mental disorder and one son was confined in this house. The family became so concerned about the possibility of the mental disorder being passed on to future generations that they decided not to have any offspring. As a result there are no descendants of that family to carry the name (and some say the curse) of Mayne.

From their amassed wealth the family made the generous donation of the land on which Queensland University was built and arranged for the University to receive the income from several other properties. The University reportedly continues to benefit from these investments to the tune of around three million dollars a year.

Bibliography

Schiller, W., Veale, A. & Harper, J. (2005). Early childhood education and care in Australia: approaches, issues, policies and research. In Bernard Spodek & Olivia N. Saracho (Eds.), *International Perspectives on Research in Early Childhood Education* (pp. 1–54). Greenwich: Information Age Publishing.

Siemon, R. (1997). *The Mayne Inheritance: a gothic tale of murder, madness and scandal across the generations. Brisbane:* University of Queensland Press.

Links

Mayne Murder
http://media.mytalk.com.au/stuff/Patrick-Mayne-Murder.pdf

Moorlands
http://www.mustdobrisbane.com/visitor-info-arts-culture-history/moorlands-Auchenflower
http://www.legacy.com.au/brisbane/History

CHAPTER 38

Teaching at Moorlands

In 1940 the Mayne family added to their generous donations to the University of Queensland and gifted Moorlands to the University. The University used it until the Second World War when it was requisitioned by the United States Army.

After the war it was sold to the Legacy War Widows and Orphans Fund and used to accommodate war widows and their children until the early sixties. At around that time it was used to house the Kindergarten Teacher's College. Subsequently it was sold to the Methodist church and for a while was a convention centre. These days Moorlands is used as office space by the Uniting Church and shares its grounds with the Wesley Private Hospital.

In retrospect its chequered history adds mawkish layers of pathos to my recollections of the few hours a week I spent at Moorlands during the sixties, teaching bright young kindergarten teacher students.

The Brisbane Kindergarten Training College occupied Moorlands in 1965 – the same year that under my mother's auspices it underwent a major reorganisation to become the Brisbane Kindergarten Teacher's College. Under her leadership the College played a significant role in researching early childhood education.

Subsequently (in 1982) the Brisbane Kindergarten Teacher's College merged with the Kelvin Grove College of advance education (formerly the Kelvin Grove Teacher's college) and the North Brisbane College of Advance Education (formerly the Kedron Park Teachers College) to form a mega-teacher-training-facility: the Brisbane College of Advanced Education. This college merged in 1990 with the Queensland Institute of Technology (formerly the Brisbane Technical College) to form the Queensland University of Technology.

These mergers were part of an Australia-wide move to turn colleges into Universities. A side effect of these mergers (or perhaps their primary aim) was to raise the stature of the colleges. Teachers at colleges became lecturers overnight and certificates became degrees. Although there is no doubt that the administration and teaching staff of these organisations rose to the challenge of raising their standards it seems likely that the overall standard of university education in Australia suffered as a result of these changes.

In preparing my lectures for the student kindergarten teachers I called on my social psychology lecture notes and some of the information in the anthropology and sociology course I had done as part of my undergraduate degree. I mapped out a curriculum that I hoped would appeal to kindergarten teacher trainees.

I really didn't know much about my students when I first started teaching them but I was impressed by the intelligence, sophistication and polish of these young women.

It was only later that I realised that this group of students was mainly drawn from the upper echelons of Brisbane society. Many of them had rich fathers and socialite mothers and had been raised to see themselves as the elite of Brisbane society.

Perhaps my mother had decided to put me in contact with these eligible young women in the hope that I might take a liking to one of them and eventually marry into high society. If so, the idea didn't take. It didn't occur to me. If I thought about it at all it was to conclude that these young ladies were definitely out of my league. Besides, they were my students and therefore off limits. I took my responsibilities as a teacher very seriously. And of course I was already taken - deeply in love and engaged to be married.

I prepared my presentations very conscientiously and my students responded positively to my efforts to teach the basics of social psychology. I provided them with a mixture of theoretical lectures and practical and experiential exercises.

Everything went swimmingly until I decided on an exercise involving a contemporary example of conflict resolution - or rather lack of it. At that time the long-running Mount Isa mines dispute was in the headlines almost daily. There had been several attempts at arbitration, which had failed. Both the union and the mine owners often made impassioned statements to the press and radio. The government made serious political capital out of attempts to control the strikers. It was a serious mess. The opportunity to engage in a meaningful class exercise was too good to miss.

I asked my students to write an essay outlining the possible reasons that this dispute had remained unresolved for so long. I encouraged them to do some background research and if possible go to primary sources – the mine management and the union officials.

In the classroom discussion that followed I soon found that my students viewed the strike through the prism of a very right wing mindset. Considering their background this is, in retrospect, unsurprising.

However I was taken by surprise. I was disconcerted that I was unable to get my students past the firm conviction that the strike was a communist plot linked to the wider plot of world domination.

This seemed a rather extreme view to me and I suggested that if they were to research the facts they may develop some sympathy for the miners and the communist point of view.

That was a big mistake. I never really recovered from what they considered to be an enormous *faux pas*. In the end I dropped that exercise and substituted something a little less threatening to capitalist ideology. But the classroom atmosphere was decidedly frosty from then on.

I learned a salutary lesson from this experience. In my future teaching I learned to read my students better and was able to anticipate where problems might arise. I learned not to meet disagreement head on and developed a more relaxed Socratic style. If there was going to be disagreement I found it better to allow my student's ideas to be challenged by other students rather than myself.

Bibliography

Schiller, W., Veale, A. & Harper, J. (2005). Early childhood education and care in Australia: approaches, issues, policies and research. In Bernard Spodek & Olivia N. Saracho (Eds.), *International Perspectives on Research in Early Childhood Education* (pp. 1–54). Greenwich: Information Age Publishing.

Links

QUT history
https://www.qut.edu.au/about/our-university/history
https://www.qut.edu.au/about/our-university/history#h2-3

CHAPTER 39

Graduation

In April 1966 I graduated with second-class honours (Division A) to congratulations all round from friends and family, a small contingent of whom turned up for the graduation ceremony. Places in the city hall were strictly limited, so it was a very intimate group consisting of my mum, my dad and my new wife who settled into folding chairs in the vast auditorium.

I hired a gown and cap – as most graduands did – and after a long wait, sweating profusely dressed up under bright lights in the summer heat, I mounted the stage. I made my obligatory cap-doffed bow to the Chancellor and shook his aching sweaty hand. I moved smartly off the stage as instructed, ceremonially moved the tassel from one side of my cap to the other, received a rolled parchment copy of my degree (selected by one official and checked by another) from a huge pile of rolled parchment balanced precariously on a trestle table.

In less than a minute I was transformed from a student into a graduate.

It must have been a mammoth task to process the hundreds of graduands, giving each one a bow, a handshake, five seconds of applause and a parchment degree. It was amazing that no one got mixed up and received the wrong degree by mistake.

I didn't realise at the time that I was in the company of graduands who would have very distinguished careers. Among them were Wayne Goss, later premier of Queensland and Keiran Cullinane later a Judge of the Supreme Court of Queensland.

However the standout at the ceremony was the graduation of Margaret Valadian - the first Aboriginal student to graduate from Queensland University. Since Margaret's surname began with a "V" her turn on stage came towards the end of the ceremony when the audience was a little bored and hands were a bit sore from clapping. As a result the applause had long since become perfunctory, hardly lasting for the time it took for each new graduate to walk off the stage.

As Margaret's name was announced the applause picked up and by the time she was shaking hands with the Chancellor it was an ovation that lasted well into the next surprised graduand's progress.

Margaret Valadian and Charlie Perkins (who graduated in 1966 from the University of New South Wales) were the first Aboriginal graduates from Australian universities and both had distinguished careers. Their graduation marked a watershed in education for Australian Aborigines. In 2014 a little over 1% of all University enrolments were Aboriginal people. While this is still well below an equitable representation of Aborigines, who comprise 2.2% of the Australian population, it is considerably better than the zero percent representation at the beginning of the sixties. This huge change has been brought about by the hard work and support of many indigenous and non-indigenous Australians. Prominent among them are Charles and Margaret who not only blazed the path for others to follow but also provided support and encouragement for subsequent Aboriginal graduates.

I made my own small contribution to this educational transformation by running training courses for indigenous counsellors and welfare workers in the seventies and eighties and various courses in remote Aboriginal settlements in the early eighties. But that's another story.

After the graduation ceremony we had a low-key celebration in a nearby coffee shop, where we sat at a small round table and I made the obligatory thank you speech to an audience of the three. I think my parents were both delightedly gob-smacked by the fact that I had actually graduated. Dad made a short, emotional speech and we toasted my graduation with fizzy soft drink and coffee.

In some ways the leisurely ceremony seemed somewhat of an anticlimax after a busy year. Arrangements for the wedding had been the usual frenzied muddle as I completed my two theses, studied for exams and frantically applied for jobs.

I applied for almost any job that was available to a person with a four-year degree in psychology. There were quite a few in the Commonwealth public service in areas ranging from industrial relations to defence, but none in clinical psychology that I could find. Nevertheless if I was going to get married and support a wife and family I would need a steady job so I applied for every position with psychology in its title.

Among others I was interviewed by a joint panel for the Commonwealth positions with representatives from every department offering psychology jobs. It was an odd experience because the panel members were not only sizing me up but were also somewhat competitive about extolling the advantages of a career in their own departments and interrupted and contradicted each other in their efforts to entice me.

I also applied for the Commonwealth Postgraduate Scholarship as did all or most of the honours students graduating that year. It was expected and encouraged by the Department to the extent that it was almost automatic. I didn't really expect that I would get a scholarship and in any case was not sure that it counted as a steady job with a decent income.

As it turned out the first offer I received was a postgraduate scholarship. The offer was from the second round, that is, it had already been turned down by somebody else and was re-offered to me. The offer came well into the New Year when I had begun to despair that I would receive any offers and I was starting to wonder what other jobs I could apply for. As a student I had worked as a farm labourer, a welder's mate and a mail sorter among other things and I started to seriously consider a career as a labourer.

The offer of a scholarship was a godsend. As a married student the pay was reasonable and the opportunity to spend a few years researching whatever I wanted was a dream come true. When I visited the department to start the process of becoming a postgraduate student I was even more delighted to find that the Department also offered a part-time tutorship to help out with living costs: extra money and the chance to teach – wonderful.

A few weeks later as I was preparing to leave the house with my family I received a phone call from the Department of Defence offering me a job there. The job probably would have involved using my skills in perception research to improve the aiming of high-tech weapons. Although it was a little later that my pacifist leanings became a solid opposition to warfare, I turned down the offer on a gut feeling that I would not like it. Besides, I had already accepted the postgraduate scholarship. Nevertheless it was very nice to feel wanted by someone else – a definite confidence boost.

It was a short phone conversation because the family was waiting for me in the car and after I had turned the job down there was not much to say. The caller was very disappointed when I told him that I had already accepted a Post Graduate Scholarship and spent a few minutes complaining about the tediously long time it takes to appoint anybody to the Department of Defence, by which time all the best people had taken jobs elsewhere.

I gathered that other Commonwealth jobs were available now that I had turned down Defence (who apparently had first option) and that my security clearance was now of the highest-level if I should wish to reconsider at any time in the future.

A high security clearance stood me in good stead in the years ahead when I needed a clearance for other Commonwealth jobs.

For now I considered myself very fortunate to be a Commonwealth Postgraduate Scholar and part-time tutor and I turned my mind to selecting a topic for my thesis and plans for my upcoming wedding.

Links

Aboriginal history
http://www.creativespirits.info/aboriginalculture/history/aboriginal-history-timeline-1900-1969#axzz3oauFRt6z
http://ab-ed.boardofstudies.nsw.edu.au/go/aboriginal-studies/timeline/timeline-1967-2007/

Keiran Cullinane
http://www.sclqld.org.au/judicial-papers/judicial-profiles/profiles/kacullinane

Indigenous Higher Education
https://www.universitiesaustralia.edu.au/uni-participation-quality/Indigenous-Higher-Education#.Vh7-GmR973R

Charles Perkins
https://en.wikipedia.org/wiki/Charles_Perkins_(Aboriginal_activist)

Margaret Valadian
http://trove.nla.gov.au/people/636060?c=people
http://www.womenaustralia.info/biogs/IMP0213b.htm
http://abceducation.net.au/videolibrary/view/margaret-valadian-82

Epilogue

At the end of 1965 I had rummaged my way through the hedge of my undergraduate years and, about to be married, I stood ready to plunge into the thicket of postgraduate studies.

Already engaged in an immense struggle to become more practical and independent of the medical establishment, Australian psychology was about to break away from the British parent body and set up independently as the Australian Psychological Society.

Australian society was also edging towards independence and along with the rest of the world was beginning to challenge conservative patterns and allow itself some freedom and creativity.

The next volume of my memoir, *Piled higher and deeper*, describes how these forces play out while I plunge into the world of postgraduate research.

Note: References, bibliographies, links and indexing

I have done my best to leave an information and ideas trail so that my reader can follow up the information presented in this book, to read further or simply to check up on what I write. You may find this information in the Bibliography and Links section at the end of each chapter.

I have used the APA style for standard references but I have adopted an idiosyncratic style designed to make web references easier to read and locate. Web sources are listed under the heading *Links* and are grouped under descriptive topic headings.

I have placed the bibliography and links list at the end of each chapter where it will be to hand as you read. This has the added advantage of keeping each list short. It has the disadvantage that it makes a particular reference harder to find in the whole book.

In ebook readers, the book can be searched to find authors, titles or indeed any word appearing in the text using the ebook reader's search function.

In order to make this feature available to all readers, a discounted ebook is available through the distributor to purchasers of the paperback, using the discount code *searchable* .

APPENDIX

Gordon Mangan's Bibliography

Parapsychology

Mangan, Gordon Lavelle. (1954, December). A PK Experiment with Thirty Dice Released for High and Low Face Targets. *Journal of Parapsychology*.

Mangan, Gordon Lavelle. (1955, March). Evidence of Displacement in a Precognitive Test. *Journal of Parapsychology*.

Mangan, Gordon Lavelle. (1957, December). An ESP Experiment with Dual-Aspect Targets Involving One Trial Day. *Journal of Parapsychology*.

Mangan, Gordon Lavelle. (1958, Spring). Parapsychology: A Science for Psychical Research? *Queen's Quarterly*.
Mangan, Gordon Lavelle. (1958). *A Review of Published Research on the Relationship of Some Personality Variables to ESP Scoring Level*. New York: Parapsychology Foundation.

Mangan, Gordon Lavelle. (1959, September). How Legitimate Are the Claims for ESP? *Australian Journal of Psychology*.

Mangan, Gordon Lavelle & Wilbur, L. C. (1956). The Relation of PK Object and Throwing Surface in Placement Tests. *Journal of Parapsychology*, 20.

Personality East and West

Mangan, Gordon L. (1967). Studies Of The Relationship Between Neo-Pavlovian Properties Of Higher Nervous Activity And Western Personality Dimensions: II. The Relation Of Mobility To Perceptual Flexibility. *Journal of Experimental Research in Personality*, 2(2), 107-116.

Mangan, G. L. (1982). *The Biology of Human Conduct: East-West Models of Temperament and Personality*. Oxford, UK: Pergamon Press.

Mangan, G. L. & Paisey, T. J. (1983). Current perspectives in neo-pavlovian temperament theory and research: A review. *Australian Journal of Psychology*, 35(3), 319-347.

White, K. D. & Mangan, G. L. (1972). Strength of the nervous system as a function of personality type and level of arousal. *Behaviour Research and Therapy,* 10(2), 139–146.

Tobacco

Bates, T., Pellett, O.L., Stough, C.K. & Mangan, G.L. (1994). The effects of smoking on simple and choice reaction time. *Psychopharmacology,* 114, 365-368.

Golding, J. F. & Mangan, G. L. (1982). Effects of Cigarette Smoking on Measures of Arousal, Response Suppression, and Excitation/Inhibition Balance. *International Journal of the Addictions,* 17(5), 793-804.

Mangan, G. L. (1982). The effects of Cigarette Smoking on Vigilance Performance. *The Journal of General Psychology*, 106(1), 77-83.

Mangan, G. L. (1983). The Effects of Cigarette Smoking on Verbal Learning and Retention, *The Journal of General Psychology*, 108(2), 203-210.

Mangan, G. & Colrain, I. (1991). Relationships Between Photic Driving, Nicotine and Memory. In Franz Adlkofer & Klaus Thurau (Eds.), *Effects of Nicotine on Biological Systems* (pp. 537-546), Basel, Switzerland: Birkhäuser.

Mangan, G. L. & Golding, J. F. (1978). An enhancement model of smoking maintenance. In R. E. Thornton (Ed.), *Smoking behaviour: physiological and psychological influences* (pp. 87-114). Edinburg: Churchill Livingstone.

Mangan, G. L. & Golding, J. F. (1983). The Effects of Smoking on Memory Consolidation. *The Journal of Psychology*, 115, 65-77.

Mangan., G. L. & Golding, J. F. (1984). *The psychopharmacology of smoking*, Cambridge: Cambridge University Press.
Stough, C., Mangan, G., Bates,T. & Pellett, O., (1994). Smoking and Raven IQ, *Psychopharmacology*, 116(3), 382-384.

Other publications

Adcock, N. & Mangan, G. L. (1970). Attention and Perceptual Learning. *The Journal of General Psychology*, 83(2), 247-254.

Bates, T. Stough, C. Mangan, G. & Pellett, O. (1995). Intelligence and complexity of the averaged evoked potential: An attentional theory. *Intelligence*, 20(1), 27-39.

Foggitt, R. H., Mangan, G. L. & Law, H., (1972). Cognitive Performance and Linguistic Codeability. *International Journal of Psychology,* 7(3), 155-161,

Mangan, G. (1945). *A Survey of the Revised Stanford-Binet Scale with New Zealand 15 and 16 Year Olds* (Unpublished master's thesis). University of New Zealand

Mangan. G. L. (1958). *Method-Of-Approach Factors in the Testing of Middle-Aged Subjects*. Journal of Gerontology, 13(1), 55-59.

Mangan, G. L. (1978). The Relationship of Mobility of Inhibition to Rate of Inhibitory Growth and Measures of Flexibility, Extraversion, and Neuroticism, *The Journal of General Psychology*, 99(2), 271-279.

G. L. Mangan & L. D. Bainbridge (Eds.). (1969). *Behaviour therapy : procedings of a symposium held by the Queensland branch of the*

Australian Psychological Society, 1967. St Lucia, Qld: University of Queensland Press.

Mangan, G., L., and Clark, J., W., 1958, Rigidity Factors In The Testing Of Middle-Aged Subjects. *Journal of Gerontology*, 13(4), 422-5.

Mangan, Gordon L. & O'Gorman, John G. (1969). Initial amplitude and rate of habituation of orienting reaction in relation to extraversion and neuroticism. *Journal of Experimental Research in Personality*, 3(4), 275-282.

Mangan, G., Murphy, G. & Farmer, R. (1980) The role of muscle tension in "repression". *Integrative Psychological and Behavioural Science*, 15(4), 172-176.

Paisey, T. H. & Mangan, G. L. (1988). Personality and conditioning with appetitive and aversive stimuli, *Personality and Individual Differences*, 9(1), 69-78

Quartermain, D. & Mangan, G. (1959). Role Of Relevance In Incidental Learning Of Verbal Material. *Perceptual and Motor Skills*, 9, 255-258.

Siddle, D.T. & Mangan, G.L. (1968). Behaviour at the point of maximum approach-avoidance conflict. *Australian Journal of Psychology*, 20(1), 27–33.

Siddle, David A. & Mangan, Gordon L. (1971). Arousability and individual differences in resistance to distraction. *Journal of Experimental Research in Personality*, 5(4), 295-303.

Siddle, David A., Morrish, Robert B., White, Kenneth D.,& Mangan, Gordon L. (1969). Relation of visual sensitivity to extraversion. *Journal of Experimental Research in Personality*, 3(4), 264-267.

Stough, C., Kerkin, B., Bates, T. & Mangan. G. (1994). Music and spatial IQ, *Personality and Individual Differences*, 17(5), 695.

White, Kenneth D., Mangan, Gordon L., Morrish, Robert B. & Siddle, David A. 1969, The relation of visual after-images to extraversion and neuroticism. *Journal of Experimental Research in Personality*, 3(4), 268-274.

Index

The ebook version can be searched using the ereader's search function.
To assist purchasers of the paperback version a discounted ebook is available through the distributor using the discount code *searchable*.

www.ingramcontent.com/pod-product-compliance
Lightning Source LLC
Chambersburg PA
CBHW022357040426
42450CB00005B/220